AN
Intellectual's
VISUAL
MISCELLANY

AN ILLUSTRATED GUIDE TO MASTERWORKS OF ART, HISTORY, LITERATURE, AND SCIENCE

DANIEL P. MURPHY, PhD

AVON, MASSACHUSETTS

Published by

Adams Media, a division of F+W Media, Inc.

57 Littlefield Street, Avon, MA 02322. U.S.A.

www.adamsmedia.com

ISBN 10: 1-4405-3881-6

ISBN 13: 978-1-4405-3881-0

eISBN 10: 1-4405-4403-4

eISBN 13: 978-1-4405-4403-3

Printed in China.

10 9 8 7 6 5 4 3 2 1

This publication is designed to provide accurate and authoritative information with regard to the subject matter covered. It is sold with the understanding that the publisher is not engaged in rendering legal, accounting, or other professional advice. If legal advice or other expert assistance is required, the services of a competent professional person should be sought.

—From a *Declaration of Principles* jointly adopted by a Committee of the American Bar Association and a Committee of Publishers and Associations

Many of the designations used by manufacturers and sellers to distinguish their product are claimed as trademarks. Where those designations appear in this book and Adams Media was aware of a trademark claim, the designations have been printed with initial capital letters.

This book is available at quantity discounts for bulk purchases.
For information, please call 1-800-289-0963.

Dedication

For Danny, who was going through Air Force Basic Training as this book was written.

Acknowledgments

Emily, Esther, Patrick, and Michael lived with the writing of this book. Without Grace Freedson, Peter Archer, and Victoria Sandbrook it would not have been.

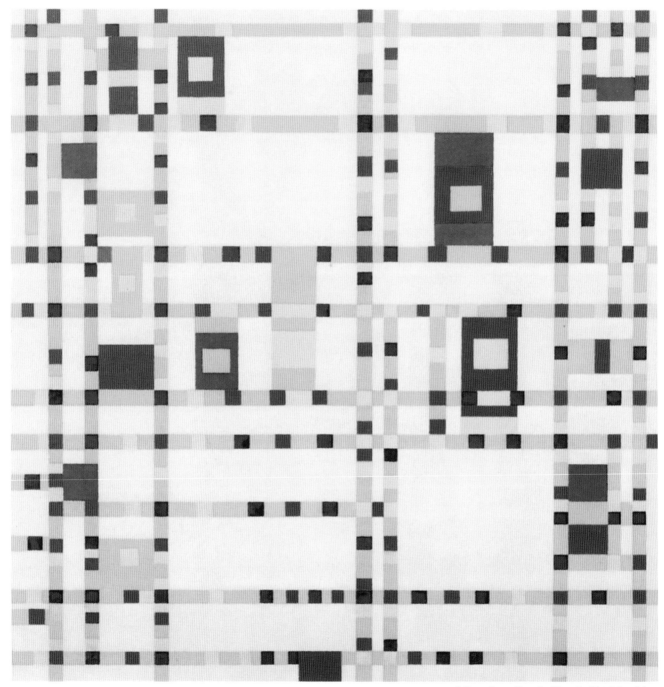

Broadway Boogie-Woogie, Piet Mondrian

Contents

■ Stamp depicting Pablo Picasso's *War*

General Introduction

One day an American soldier engaged the painter Pablo Picasso in a discussion of art. The soldier observed that he did not like abstract art because it was too unrealistic. Moving on to other topics, the soldier produced a photograph of his girlfriend. Picasso looked the picture over and burst out, "My, is she really that small?"

In this anecdote, Picasso does more than attempt to teach his interlocutor a lesson about visual literalness; he touches on the mysterious heart of images and the nature of visual representation. Lurking in the background of the exchange between Picasso and the soldier is a fundamental divide over what a picture is and what it should do. The soldier believed that a painting should as closely as possible resemble its subject. He believed that the point of a painting was to allow viewers to see what any passerby might see,

the subject recognizably ensconced in the quotidian world. Implicit in the soldier's view is an epistemology, a conviction that we can know what we see and see what we know.

Picasso embodies a different worldview. In his art, Picasso was a pioneer of Cubism. Embracing abstraction, the Cubists painted their subjects simultaneously from multiple perspectives. Picasso's work was a visual manifestation of a Modernist understanding that "reality" is a complicated and elusive concept. His notion of seeing was bound up in a relativistic world where everything depends upon your point of view. Picasso expressed this insight very succinctly later in his career when a wealthy American woman visited his studio looking for a painting to purchase. Standing before one of his abstractions, she asked, "What does this picture represent?" Picasso replied, "Two hundred thousand dollars."

But Picasso did have something in common with the soldier. He shared a desire to see an object, even if he wanted to see things in a new way. What he also recognized, together with the soldier, is that an image, whether realistic or abstract, has a power. A picture speaks to us. It is a transitory mirror on the world, a moment that has been captured and transferred to something physically immediate. This lies at the heart of the primitive belief that a photograph can steal one's soul, as well as the old expression "A picture is worth a thousand words." People care about pictures because pictures are important. The way something is portrayed shapes both memory and understanding. This is why the debate between Picasso and the soldier was significant; images are consequential and both men knew it.

Pictures are important to this book. In the following pages, images will speak loudly. They are as much a part of the text as the words. The power in each is complementary. Here pictures and words exist in dynamic counterpoint, illuminating and commenting on each other. The word "visual" in the title is taken very seriously. We hope that the possessor of this book will "see" as well as "read" it.

This is a book to be dipped into more than once. Some days it will be the pictures that speak, other times the text, or perhaps they both will act together in producing an original insight. This book is intended to be a work constantly in progress.

What is on offer is a miscellany, a collection of the important, the interesting, and occasionally the odd. This is a book that we hope is entertaining; we believe that sometimes this book will be useful as well.

We have embedded a lot of information in this miscellany: pictures, text, lists of related works. The format is handy and attractive. Though hardly exhaustive, this book provides a brief overview of some important things an educated person ought to know. As such, it is a practical antidote to the centripetal tendencies of modern knowledge. Contemporary culture is growing increasingly fragmented. Where once there were three television networks, viewers now choose between hundreds of possibilities. Top 30 radio stations have given way to stations with specialized programming. The Internet promises access to the whole range of human learning, but it does so by giving users an overwhelming mass of possibilities, many providing trustworthy information, some not. Our visual miscellany helps one thread a path through this daunting maze of data. It offers an engaging lifeline to people looking to attain cultural literacy without surrendering to the encyclopedia.

Last but not least, this is the sort of book that we would like to own. The interplay of picture and text has been exciting as we worked to bring this to you. We enjoyed putting this visual miscellany together. We hope that you will equally enjoy taking it (metaphorically) apart.

Chapter 1

Painting and Sculpture

Pope Benedict VIII was famous for his pride. Nothing but the best would do for him. When he wanted to commission some paintings for St. Peter's Basilica in Rome, the Pope sent one of his courtiers north to Tuscany to get samples from the great painters of Siena and Florence. Because of the importance of the prospective job, all these men provided drawings showcasing their skills. When the courtier arrived at the workshop of Giotto, he explained his mission and asked Giotto for a drawing to take back to Rome. Giotto took a piece of paper and dipped a pen in red ink. Holding his arm to his side to make a compass of it, Giotto drew a perfect circle. Smiling, he offered this to the courtier, saying, "Here is the drawing." The courtier was taken aback by this and asked, "Am I to have no other drawing than this?" Giotto responded, "This is enough and too much."

The courtier returned to Rome and showed the drawings to the Pope, including the circle drawn by Giotto. When the Pope heard the full story of the drawing, he and his advisors realized that Giotto's abilities were greater than all of his contemporaries. Before long a proverb began to circulate: "You are rounder than the O of Giotto." Giotto was awarded the Pope's commission and painted a series of masterpieces for St. Peter's Basilica. The story of Giotto's circle illuminates the skill and often deceptive simplicity that lies behind so much artistic creativity.

▌*The Calf-Bearer*

Archaic and Ancient Greek Art

Around the year 800 B.C. Greece emerged from a dark age. City-states known as *poleis* (singular *polis*) grew and prospered economically, thus making possible the dawning of Archaic Greek art around the middle of the seventh century B.C. Sculptors carved statues from stone or cast them in bronze to represent local heroes or gods, divine beings whom the Greeks created in their image.

Statues of nude young men (*kouros*) and clothed young women (*kore*) were heavily influenced by Egyptian models but demonstrated the distinctively Greek fascination with the human body. Their smiles reflect, perhaps, the optimism of an expanding civilization. For the Greeks, pottery vessels could be works of art as well as practical necessities. Incised outlines allowed painters to bring a new dynamism to the surfaces of black-figure pottery.

Statue of a *kouros* carrying a ram, dated ca. 600 B.C.

Peplos kore

Collection of Greek vases

▌ *Doryphoros*

▌ *Hermes and the Infant Dionysus*

▌ Frontal view of the *Colonna Venus*, an ancient replica of the Aphrodite of Knidos by Praxiteles

The Beauty of Classical Greece

The fifth century B.C. was a time of cultural splendor in Greece, when the proud Greek *poleis* reached the pinnacle of their wealth and power. It was also when Greek artists displayed remarkable skill in portraying idealized evocations of the human form. Classical Greek sculptors such as Phidias and Praxiteles created works that became the standard of beauty in the Western world for more than 2,000 years.

 Lysippos

▌ *Laocoön and His Sons*

The Heritage of Alexander

Alexander the Great inaugurated the Hellenistic period when he conquered an enormous empire that included not only Greece but also the Persian lands to the east. Greek culture and art spread from Egypt in the west to India in the east. Hellenistic artists found themselves in great demand by the royal dynasts who came after Alexander and beautified their realms.

Hellenistic art retained the technical virtuosity of the previous Classical Age, but the range of subjects widened. A new realism emerged, with a more naturalistic portrayal of people who did not meet the standard of physical perfection. Hellenistic art was also more dramatically charged than its predecessors, often depicting scenes of intense emotional power.

Winged Victory of Samothrace

Venus de Milo

The Dying Gaul

▮ Herculaneum, Italy

Treasures of Roman Painting

As might be expected, Roman painting was heavily influenced by Greek models as the Romans expanded their rule across the Mediterranean. Unlike the Greeks, though, the Romans experimented with perspective in paintings of natural and urban landscapes. Almost all of the surviving examples of Roman painting come from the walls of buildings in Pompeii and Herculaneum, buried and preserved in volcanic ash by the eruption of Vesuvius in A.D. 79.

LIST OF WORKS

▮ *Venus and Mars*, House of the Citharist, Pompeii

▮ *Jason Recognized by Pelias*, Pompeii

▮ *Iphigenia in Tauris*, Pompeii

▮ *Hercules, Nessus, and Deianira*, House of the Centaur, Pompeii

▮ *Hercules and Telephus*, Basilica, Herculaneum

▮ *Hercules and Omphale*, House of the Mosaic Atrium, Herculaneum

▮ *Two Women*, Boscoreale

■ Ancient fresco in Pompeii

■ Detail of ancient fresco in Pompeii

■ *Lararium of the Termopolium*

▮ Replica of Sutton Hoo ship-burial helmet © The Trustees of the British Museum

The First Stirrings of Medieval Civilization

With the fall of the Western Roman Empire in the fifth century, Germanic tribes swept across Western Europe. With them, they brought geometric and abstract styles of working with jewelry and metal. In Britain and Ireland, Celtic traditions of elabo-rately stylized decoration fused with Germanic influences and Christian forms inherited from the Roman Empire to create a distinctive artistic style.

LIST OF WORKS

- Treasure of Gourdon, Bibliothèque nationale de France, Paris

- Sutton Hoo Shoulder Clasps, Sutton Hoo, Suffolk, England

- Visigothic Pair of Eagle Fibulae, Walters Art Museum, Baltimore, Maryland

- Iron Crown of Lombardy, Cathedral of Monza, Milan

- Fuller Brooch, British Museum, London

- *Book of Durrow*, Trinity College Library, Dublin

- *Book of Kells*, Trinity College, Dublin

- Tara Brooch, National Museum of Ireland, Dublin

- Ardagh Chalice, National Museum of Ireland, Dublin

- Celtic Cross, Monasterboice, Ireland

- Gokstad Ship, Viking Ship Museum, Oslo, Norway

- Gundestrup Cauldron, National Museum of Denmark, Copenhagen

- Stora Hammars Stones, Gotland, Sweden

- Lorsch Gospels, Biblioteca Apostolica Vaticana, Rome

- *Codex Aureus of St. Emmeram*, Bayerische Staatsbibliothek, Munich

■ **Top:** Celtic cross
■ **Bottom:** Close up of Celtic design

■ Page from *Book of Kells*

Romanesque and Gothic Painting

After the year A.D. 1000, Western Europe entered a period of economic, political, and religious dynamism that fostered an age of intense artistic creativity. The expressive imagery of Romanesque painting freely departed from its classical models. Gothic painting, emerging around A.D. 1200, emphasized realism and a greater depth of perspective when depicting people.

LIST OF WORKS

■ Winchester Bible, Winchester Cathedral Library, England

■ *Psalter of Saint Louis*, Bibliothèque nationale de France, Paris

■ *Chapel of the Holy Cross* by Theodoric of Prague, Karlštejn Castle, Czech Republic

■ *Merode Altarpiece* by Robert Campin, Metropolitan Museum of Art, New York

■ *Ghent Altarpiece* by Jan van Eyck, Saint Bavo's Cathedral, Ghent, Belgium

■ *St Albans Psalter*

■ *Hours of Catherine of Cleves*

■ Limbourg Brothers, *Les Très Riches Heures du Duc de Berry: Juin*

▌Giotto, *Kiss of Judas*

▌Giotto, *Stigmata of St. Francis*

Medieval Painting

Cimabue (ca. 1240–ca. 1302), a Florentine painter nicknamed Ox-head, was the outstanding painter of his day. His work encouraged a turn toward greater realism. Giotto (1267–1337), a sculptor and architect as well as a painter, also participated in the movement toward a more realistic, less stylized art. In his naturalism and his ability to convincingly delineate pictorial space, Giotto is an important precursor to the Renaissance. It is a mark of their importance that both Cimabue and Giotto were mentioned approvingly by Dante in his *Divine Comedy*.

▍ Cimabue, Baptistery of Florence and detail of mosaic

▍ Cimabue, *Maestà*

▌Scene from the *Khamsa of Nizami*, Persian, 1539–1543

▌Moorish tiles

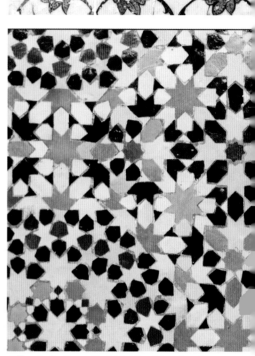

▌**Top to bottom:** Turkish blue tiles; floral pattern in tiles from Meknes Medina, Morocco

Islamic Art and Design

From the seventh century, Islam spread outward from Arabia, leading to the emergence of a distinctive and vital artistic tradition. Because Muslims believe that picturing human beings for religious purposes is idolatrous and sinful, much Islamic art is devoted to the elaboration of abstract patterns and calligraphy. Depictions of humans and animals often appear in works intended for private or secular purposes.

▌ Masaccio's *San Giovenale Triptych (Cascia Altarpiece)*

The Florentine Renaissance

The early fifteenth century saw a "rebirth," or "renaissance" of interest in Classical Greek and Roman models in art. The wealthy city of Florence on the Italian peninsula was home to such great artists as Masaccio (1401–1428), who renewed the practice of painting nudes and advanced the use of perspective, and Donatello (ca. 1386–1466), whose sculptures showed a Classical appreciation for human beauty.

LIST OF WORKS

▌ *The Expulsion of Adam and Eve* by Masaccio, Brancacci Chapel, Santa Maria del Carmine, Florence

▌ *David* by Donatello, Museo Nazionale del Bargello, Florence

▌ *The Battle of San Romano* by Paolo Uccello, National Gallery, London

▌ *The Birth of Venus* by Sandro Botticelli, Uffizi Gallery of Florence

▌ *The Last Judgment* by Fra Angelico, San Marco, Florence

Top left: *Coronation of the Virgin by Angelico,* Uffizi Gallery of Florence

Bottom left: Botticelli's *Madonna of the Magnificat*

Donatello's statue *Saint Mark*

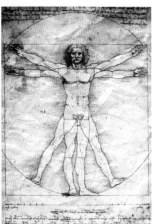

▌**This page top and left to right:** Da Vinci's *The Last Supper;* Da Vinci's *The Mona Lisa*; Da Vinci's *Vetruvian Man*; Raphael's *Saint George and the Dragon*

▌**Opposite page top to bottom:** Detail of *The Last Judgment* by Michelangelo, Sistine Chapel, Vatican City; Alberti's Trevi fountain

The High Renaissance

By the late fifteenth century, Rome had replaced Florence as the center of Renaissance creativity, as the new artistic vision spread throughout Italy and beyond. The polymath genius Leonardo da Vinci (1452–1519) experimented with materials and innovative techniques to capture "the intention of man's soul." Michelangelo (1475–1564), an architect, sculptor, and painter, explored the dramatic possibilities of the human form, while Raphael (1483–1520) painted works of classically harmonious beauty.

LIST OF WORKS

- *Annunciation* by Leonardo da Vinci, Uffizi Gallery of Florence
- *The Virgin of the Rocks* by Leonardo da Vinci, Louvre, Paris
- *John the Baptist* by Leonardo da Vinci, Louvre, Paris
- *Pietà* by Michelangelo, St. Peter's Basilica, Vatican City, Rome
- *David* by Michelangelo, Gallery of the Accademia di Belle Arti, Florence
- *Sistine Madonna* by Raphael, Old Masters Picture Gallery, Dresden, Germany
- *The School of Athens* by Raphael, Apostolic Palace, Vatican City, Rome
- *Sleeping Venus* by Giorgione, Old Masters Picture Gallery, Dresden
- *St. Francis in Ecstasy* by Giovanni Bellini, Frick Collection, New York City
- *Assumption of the Virgin* by Titian, Basilica di Santa Maria Gloriosa dei Frari, Venice

The Northern Renaissance and Beyond

Northern European artists such as the Flemish painter Jan van Eyck (ca. 1380–1441) were notable for their realism and intense dedication to detail in their paintings. Albrecht Dürer (1471–1528) imbibed lessons on perspective and proportion from the Italian Renaissance, and combined these techniques with a traditional Northern European attention to detail in his paintings and engravings. Hans Holbein (ca. 1497–1543), court painter to the English King Henry VIII, was the Northern Renaissance master of portraiture. A century later, mercantile prosperity in the Netherlands funded the Dutch Golden Age painting. Rembrandt van Rijn (1606–1669) combined realism with emotional insight, while Jan (or Johannes) Vermeer (1632–1675) expressed a fascination with the manifestations of light in everyday life.

▍**Top to bottom:** Rembrandt's *The Three Crosses* and *The Nativity*

▌ Holbein's *Portrait of Henry VIII*

▌ Holbein's *Portrait of Queen Catherine Parr*

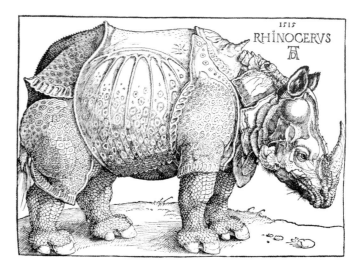

▌ **Above:** Dürer's *The Rhinoceros* engraving; **Left:** Vermeer's *Girl with a Pearl Earring*

■ *Supper at Emmaus* by Caravaggio, 1601

The Light of the Baroque

Baroque art, which emerged in Italy around 1600, was closely associated with the Roman Catholic Counter-Reformation. The Counter-Reformation saw art as a useful adjunct in the struggle for people's souls, drawing them back to the Catholic Church. Such art was colorful and dramatic, often depicting religious themes or scenes from mythology and history. Caravaggio (1571–1610) used stark contrasts of light and dark to heighten the emotional intensity of his paintings. Peter Paul Rubens (1577–1640) was notable for his lush palette and full-bodied figures, and Gianlorenzo Bernini (1598–1680) combined piety with sensuous motion in his sculptures.

▌*Saint Sebastian* by Titian

▌*Portrait of the Infanta Maria Theresa of Spain* by Velázquez

▌Bernini, Angels, Ponte Sant'Angelo ("Holy Angel Bridge"), Rome, 1668

▌Bernini, *Piazza Navona*, Rome

▌Lorrain, *Seaport at Sunset*, 1639

Rococo in France

In reaction to the grandiosity of Baroque art, in the eighteenth century artists created the style known as Rococo art. These artists stressed curved lines and softer colors, and for subject matter they turned to romantic and playful themes. French artists took the lead in developing the Rococo style: Antoine Watteau (1684–1721) idealized the aristocratic life, while Jean-Honoré Fragonard (1732–1806) painted erotically charged scenes of delicate beauty.

▌Antoine Watteau, *Pierrot*, 1718–1719

▌ Fragonard, *The Progress of Love Series*, 1771

▌**Top:** Élisabeth Vigée-Lebrun self-portrait
▌**Bottom:** Étienne Maurice Falconet, monument to Peter the Great

LIST OF WORKS

▌ *Pilgrimage on the Isle of Cythera* by Antoine Watteau, Louvre, Paris

▌ *Gersaint's Shopsign* by Antoine Watteau, Charlottenburg Palace, Berlin

▌ *Pygmalion and Galatée* by Étienne Maurice Falconet, Hermitage Museum, Saint Petersburg

▌ *Portrait of Marie-Louise O'Murphy* by François Boucher, Wallraf-Richartz Museum, Cologne

▌ *Portrait of Madame de Pompadour* by François Boucher, Wallace Collection, London

▌ *The Bath of Venus* by François Boucher, National Gallery of Art, Washington, D.C.

▌ *Portrait of Marie Antoinette* by Louise-Elisabeth Vigée-Lebrun, Château de Versailles, Versailles

▌ *Blind Man's Bluff* by Jean-Honoré Fragonard, Toledo Museum of Art, Toledo, Ohio

▌ *The Swing* by Jean-Honoré Fragonard, Wallace Collection, London

▌ *A Young Girl Reading* by Jean-Honoré Fragonard, National Gallery of Art, Washington, D.C.

■ **This page top to bottom:** Gainsborough's *Mr. and Mrs. Robert Andrews*, ca. 1748–1750; Gainsborough's *The Blue Boy*, 1770

■ **Opposite page top to bottom:** Hogarth's *Before* and *After* engravings; Gainsborough's *The Lottery*

English Pastoralism

Influenced by what was known as the "French taste," British artists plunged into the Rococo movement. English portrait painters were especially inspired by the Rococo aesthetic. Thomas Gainsborough (1727–1788) and Sir Joshua Reynolds (1723–1792) helped create a golden age of English portraiture. Satirical artist William Hogarth (1697–1764) defended the curved line as the source of all beauty.

LIST OF WORKS

■ **Above:** Goya, *The Nude Maja*, ca. 1800; **Opposite page:** *The Clothed Maja*, ca. 1803

The Romantic Revolution

Romantics reacted against the neo-Classical revival of the late eighteenth century. Instead, they stressed the individuality of their artistic vision. Rather than Classical restraint, they embraced vivid color and strong feeling. Typical Romantic subjects were scenes of nature or depictions of dramatic events in history. Francisco Goya (1746–1828) ranged from intimate portraits to evocations of the horrors of war, while Théodore Géricault (1791–1824) painted moments of emotional and physical extremity.

■ Goya, *The Sleep of Reason Produces Monsters*, ca. 1797

▍Géricault, *Raft of the Medusa, 1818–1819*

▍Friedrich, *Wanderer above the Sea of Fog*

❚ Rodin's *The Thinker* and *The Kiss*

Nineteenth-Century European Art

Around 1850, the inroads of the Industrial Revolution and the emergence of a mass commercial culture inspired a number of artists to abandon Romanticism for what they believed was a more objective approach to art. Realists attempted to depict ordinary people in their everyday life as truthfully as possible.

The French painters Gustave Courbet (1819–1877) and Jean-François Millet (1814–1875) portrayed laborers and peasants at work. The sculptor Auguste Rodin (1840–1917) created intensely powerful figures in an often stunningly realistic style.

Top: Francisco Pradilla Ortiz, *Doña Juana "la Loca,"* Museo del Prado, Madrid, Spain

Bottom: Francisco Pradilla Ortiz, *The Capitulation of Granada: Boabdil Confronts Ferdinand and Isabella*, 1882

▌John James Audubon, *Northern Cardinal*

The American Spirit

American art in the nineteenth century reflected the concerns of a new nation expanding across a vast frontier. Many painters were inspired by America's natural grandeur. Thomas Cole (1801–1848) founded the Hudson River School of landscape painters in the 1820s. John James Audubon (1785–1851) made naturalism an art in his depictions of birds. George Catlin (1796–1872) captured the vanishing Native American on canvas, while George Caleb Bingham (1811–1879) memorably evoked pioneer life. Later in the century, James Whistler (1834–1903) attained an international reputation as a portraitist.

▌**Top to bottom:** Edward Hopper, *Girl at Sewing Machine;* George Catlin, *Sioux War Council*

▮ Morris Hunt, *The Drummer Boy* and *Study for Fortune*

LIST OF WORKS

▮ *Distant View of Niagara Falls* by Thomas Cole, Art Institute of Chicago

▮ *White Cloud, Head Chief of the Iowas* by George Catlin, National Gallery of Art, Washington, D.C.

▮ *Fur Traders Descending the Missouri* by George Caleb Bingham, Metropolitan Museum of Art, New York

▮ *Daniel Boone Escorting Settlers Through the Cumberland Gap* by George Caleb Bingham, Washington University Gallery of Art, St. Louis, Missouri

▮ *The Gulf Stream* by Winslow Homer, Metropolitan Museum of Art, New York

▮ *The Gross Clinic* by Thomas Eakins, Philadelphia Museum of Art

▮ *The Swimming Hole* by Thomas Eakins, Amon Carter Museum, Fort Worth, Texas

▮ *The Child's Bath* by Mary Cassatt, Art Institute of Chicago

▮ *Mother of Pearl and Silver: The Andalusian* by James Whistler, National Gallery of Art, Washington, D.C.

▮ *Arrangement in Grey and Black No. 1 (Whistler's Mother)* by James Whistler, Musée d'Orsay, Paris

▮ Thomas Cole, *The Course of Empire: The Consummation*

The Pre-Raphaelites

A group of English painters led by William Holman Hunt (1827–1910), John Everett Millais (1829–1896), and Dante Gabriel Rossetti (1828–1882) launched the Pre-Raphaelite Brotherhood in 1848. Artistic rebels, they rejected the conventional academic painting of their day, which they believed was rooted in the example of the great Renaissance painter Raphael. Instead, they looked to artists before Raphael for inspiration, to the great Italian and Flemish painters of the fifteenth century. The Pre-Raphaelites brought a Romantic sensibility to their work, emphasizing a careful study of nature, brilliant color, and a taste for medieval themes.

LIST OF WORKS

Early Photography

In 1826, the French inventor Joseph Nicéphore Niepce (1765–1833) created the first photograph, a view out the window of his home. To get this image, he exposed a plate of pewter coated with a petroleum derivative for eight hours. To refine the photographic process, Niepce collaborated with Louis Daguerre (1787–1851). Following Niepce's death, Daguerre used silver salts to reduce exposure times to ten minutes. The French government purchased the rights to the "daguerreotype," and published the process to the world in 1839. Photography was born.

▍ **Top to bottom:** Joseph Nicéphore Niepce, *View from the Window at Le Gras;* Julia Margaret Cameron, *Sir John Herschel with Cap,* 1867 © ImageState RM / *www.fotosearch.com*

Impressions of Light

Impressionist art emerged in France in the 1870s. In an era when photography challenged the traditional artistic imperative to capture reality, the Impressionists abandoned academic approaches to pictorial representation. Camille Pissarro (1830–1903) expressed the new aesthetic when he wrote: "Don't proceed according to rules and principles, but paint what you observe and feel. Paint generously and unhesitatingly, for it is best not to lose the first impression." Impressionists brilliantly explored the interplay of light and color.

Opposite page left to right: Monet, *Rouen Cathedral*, 1894; *Water Lilies,* 1914. **This page clockwise from top left:** Manet, *Spring*, 1881; Degas, *Before the Rehearsal*, 1880; Cassatt, *The Cup of Tea*, 1880; Cailleboitte, *Le pont de l'Europe*, 1877; Renoir, *Luncheon of the Boating Party,* 1881

LIST OF WORKS

▌ *Impression, Sunrise* by Claude Monet, Musée Marmottan Monet, Paris

▌ *Family Reunion* by Frédéric Bazille, Musée d'Orsay, Paris

▌ *Paris Street, Rainy Day* by Gustave Caillebotte, Art Institute of Chicago

▌ *Dancers at the Bar* by Edgar Degas, Phillips Collection, Washington, D.C.

▌ *Sunset at Ivry* by Armand Guillaumin, Musée d'Orsay, Paris

▌ *The Luncheon on the Grass* by Édouard Manet, Musée d'Orsay, Paris

▌ *The Cattle Ridge at L'Hermitage* by Camille Pissarro, National Gallery, London

▌ *Street in Moret* by Alfred Sisley, Art Institute of Chicago

▌ *Dance at Le Moulin de la Galette* by Pierre-Auguste Renoir, Musée d'Orsay, Paris

Post-Impressionism

The Post-Impressionists shared the Impressionist interest in color and light, but worried that the new painting was sacrificing order and structure. Paul Cezanne (1839–1906) sought to see objects as constructs of natural forms, to "treat nature by the cylinder, the sphere, the cone." Georges Seurat (1859–1891) created visual harmony through Pointillism, applying paint in dots of color. Vincent van Gogh (1853–1890) used vigorous brushwork to shape paint in arcs of brilliant color.

LIST OF WORKS

▮ *The Card Players* by Paul Cezanne, Musée d'Orsay, Paris

▮ *The Bathers* by Paul Cezanne, Philadelphia Museum of Art

▮ *A Sunday Afternoon on the Island of La Grande Jatte* by Georges Seurat, Art Institute of Chicago

▮ *The Eiffel Tower* by Georges Seurat, California Palace of the Legion of Honor, San Francisco

▮ *The Talisman* by Paul Serusier, Musée d'Orsay, Paris

▮ *Still Life: Vase with Twelve Sunflowers* by Vincent van Gogh, Neue Pinakothek, Munich

▌**Opposite page:** Cezanne, *Monte Sainte Victoire,* 1885–1887. **This page clockwise from top left:** Gaugin, *When Will You Marry?,* 1892; Van Gogh, *Starry Night,* 1888; Seurat, *Bathing at Asnieres,* 1883

▌**Left to right:** Toulouse-Lautrec, *The Toilette,* 1889; Toulouse-Lautrec, *La Goulue Arriving at Moulin Rouge with Two Women,* 1892; Vuillard, *Child in a Room,* 1900; Vuillard, *The Art Dealers,* 1908

The Color of Reality

The Post-Impressionists wanted to get beyond surface representation and express their subjective feelings. Their emotional state might literally color their depictions of reality. This led to a pictorial abstraction that made them the progenitors of modern art. Henri de Toulouse-Lautrec (1864–1901) painted vivid evocations of Parisian nightlife, while Paul Gauguin (1848–1903) celebrated primitivism in the South Seas. Henri Matisse (1869–1954) abandoned naturalism for the expressive use of color. Describing a portrait, he wrote, "I did not create a woman, I made a painting."

LIST OF WORKS

The Scream of Expressionism

In the early twentieth century, many painters searched for even more intensive ways of expressing their subjective visions of the world by freely distorting reality in their work. One inspiration for the Expressionists was the Norwegian painter Edvard Munch (1863–1944), whose famous work *The Scream* (1893) captured raw emotion on canvas. As Munch himself wrote of his masterpiece, "I was stretched to the limit—nature was screaming in my blood."

LIST OF WORKS

- *The Sick Child* by Edvard Munch, Tate Gallery, London
- *Houses at Murnau* by Wassily Kandinsky, Art Institute of Chicago
- *Judith and the Head of Holofernes* by Gustav Klimt, Belvedere Palace, Vienna
- *The Kiss* by Gustav Klimt, Belvedere Palace, Vienna
- *Self-Portrait* by Egon Schiele, Leopold Museum, Vienna
- *The Bride of the Wind* by Oskar Kokoschka, Kunstmuseum, Basel, Switzerland
- *Girl Under a Japanese Parasol* by Ernst Ludwig Kirchner, Kunstsammlung Nordrhein-Westfalen, Dusseldorf, Germany
- *Horse in a Landscape* by Franz Marc, Museum Folkwang, Essen, Germany
- *Lady in a Green Jacket* by August Macke, Museum Ludwig, Cologne, Germany
- *The Ice Hole* by Marsden Hartley, New Orleans Museum of Art
- *Crucifixion* by Georges Rouault, Minneapolis Institute of Arts
- *Portrait of a Young Girl* by Emil Nolde, Hermitage Museum, St. Petersburg
- *Suicide* by George Grosz, Tate Gallery, London
- *Self-Portrait with a Carnation* by Otto Dix, Institute of the Arts, Detroit, Michigan
- *Landscape with Yellow Nudes* by Otto Mueller, Museum of Modern Art, New York

■ **Opposite page left to right:** Munch, *The Madonna,* 1894–95, Munch, *The Scream,* 1893; Kandinsky, *The Blue Horseman,* 1903; **This page top to bottom:** Kandinsky, *Improvisation "Klamm,"* 1914; Heckel, *Spring,* 1918

▌Picasso, *Les Demoiselles d'Avignon,* 1907

Cubism and Geometric Art

With Cubism, modern art embraced abstraction. Moving away from a conventional representation of forms, artists disassembled objects, painting them simultaneously from different viewpoints. In cubist paintings, perspective became wholly subjective and reality was reimagined. Pablo Picasso (1881–1973) and Georges Braque (1882–1963) began experimenting with this new approach to the canvas in 1908. A critic described a painting by Braque as being "full of little cubes," thus giving the movement its name.

LIST OF WORKS

- *Man with a Guitar* by Georges Braque, Museum of Modern Art, New York

- *The Large Horse* by Raymond Duchamp-Villon, Museum of Fine Arts, Houston

- *Nudes in the Forest* by Fernand Leger, Kröller-Müller Museum, Otterlo, Netherlands

- *Woman with Animals* by Albert Gleizes, Solomon R. Guggenheim Museum, New York

- *The Conquest of the Air* by Roger de La Fresnaye, Museum of Modern Art, New York

- *Ma Jolie* by Pablo Picasso, Museum of Modern Art, New York

- *The Guitar Player* by Pablo Picasso, Musée National d'Art Moderne, Paris

- *The Sunblind* by Juan Gris, Tate Gallery, London

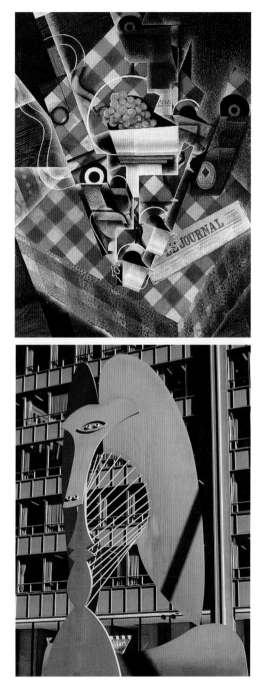

▌**Top to bottom:** Juan Gris, *Still Life with Checked Tablecloth,* 1915; Picasso, sculpture donated to the people of Chicago, 1963–67

▌Dalí, *Swans Reflecting Elephants,* 1937 © Bridgeman-Giraudon / Art Resource, NY

Dada and Surrealism

The First World War (1914–18) devastated Europe. In addition to millions of casualties and massive destruction, the Great War challenged the cherished Western conviction that the world was a fundamentally rational place, steadily marching upward. Dada artists believed that the war demonstrated the essential meaninglessness of life; thus, in their art they embraced absurdity. Out of Dadaism emerged Surrealism. The Surrealists wanted to tap the unplumbed depths of the unconscious to bring a new "absolute reality" to their art.

LIST OF WORKS

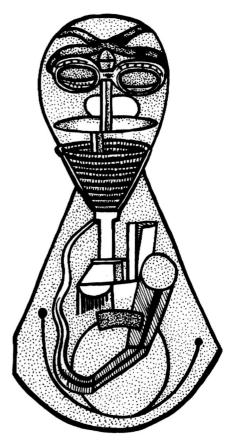

▮ **Top to bottom:** Max Ernst, abstract detail; Juan Miró, detail of mosaic in the Barcelona airport

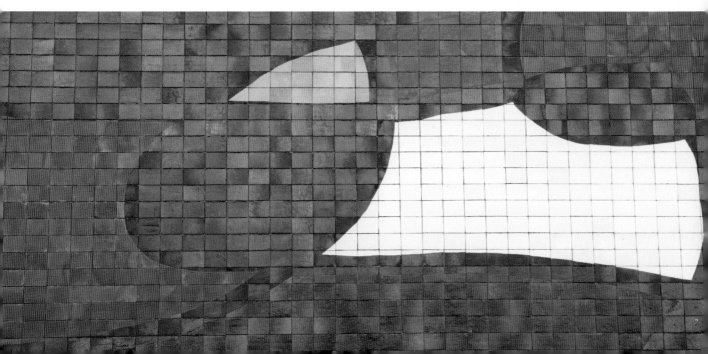

Art of China– The Terracotta Army

In 221 B.C., Ying Zheng, the King of Qin, conquered the last of his rival monarchs, ending the Warring States Period in China. Renaming himself Qin Shi Huang, the First Emperor, he became an efficient, if brutal, ruler. Qin Shi Huang suppressed freedom of thought, but reorganized governmental administration and erected the first Great Wall of China. He also constructed a massive burial complex for himself at Mount Li, near modern Xi'an. In addition to his tomb mound, four large pits were built containing a terracotta army to accompany the emperor into the next world upon his death in 210 B.C.

FACTS ABOUT THE TERRACOTTA ARMY

- The Terracotta Army was discovered by peasants digging a well in 1974.

- The Qin emperor's mausoleum contains 8,000 terracotta soldiers, individualized through a construction process using interchangeable parts.

- The mausoleum also contains 150 cavalry horses and 130 chariots driven by 520 horses.

- Swords found in the mausoleum were rust-free and sharp.

- The emperor's tomb has not been opened and may contain great treasures.

Centuries of Chinese Art

Only ancient Egyptian civilization can rival that of China for continuity through time. For 4,000 years, Chinese art has been heavily influenced by a reverence for nature. This tendency was reinforced by the great philosophical and religious systems that developed in China. Confucianism, Taoism, and Buddhism all encouraged an ethical humanism and living in harmony with nature. Chinese artists excelled in many genres for thousands of years, from painting to sculpture to printmaking.

LIST OF WORKS

▪ Bronze Bell, Eastern Zhou Dynasty, Museum for East Asian Art, Berlin

▪ *Spring Excursion* by Zhan Ziqian, Sui Dynasty, Palace Museum, Beijing

▪ *Preface to the Poems Collected from the Orchard Pavilion* by Wang Xizhi, Tang Dynasty copy, Palace Museum, Beijing

▪ *Night-Shining White* by Han Gan, Tang Dynasty, Metropolitan Museum of Art, New York

▪ *Along the River During the Qinming Festival* by Zhang Zeduan, Song Dynasty, Palace Museum, Beijing

▪ *Dwelling in the Fuchun Mountains* by Huang Gongwang, Yuan Dynasty, National Palace Museum, Taipei

▪ *Wintry Trees* by Wen Zhengming, Ming Dynasty, British Museum, London

▪ *Master Shi Planting Pines* by Shi Tao, Qing Dynasty, National Palace Museum, Taipei

▌**Opposite page left to right:** Tang Dynasty fresco; ancient Chinese calligraphy; **This page:** Su Hanchen (ca. 1130–1160), *Children Playing in Autumn Courtyard* (detail of scroll painting)

▌**Top to bottom:** Eitoku, guardian lions; Shunsho, *The Actor Segawa Kikunojo II*

The Fine Arts in Japan

Japan's artistic tradition reaches back to the first people who settled on the islands. High art in Japan was initially indebted to Chinese civilization. The introduction of Buddhism in the sixth century had a profound effect on Japanese art. From the ninth century on, Japanese art became increasingly distinctive. By the nineteenth century, Japanese art was influencing Western artists, and the works of Utagawa Hiroshige (1797–1858) inspired Claude Monet and Vincent van Gogh.

▌**Top:** Hokusai, *Under a Wave off Kanagawa*, 1830–32; **Bottom left:** Hiroshige, *Crossing at Suda*, 1830s; **Bottom right:** Hiroshige, *Peonies*, n.d.

LIST OF WORKS

▌*Haniwa Soldier*, Kofun Period, Tokyo National Museum

▌*Bodhisattva*, Asuka Period, Chujugi Temple, Nara, Japan

▌*The Tale of the Great Minister Ban* by Tokiwa Mitsunaga, Heian Period, Idemitsu Museum of Arts, Tokyo

▌*Nio Guardian* by Unkei, Kamakura Period, Todaiji Temple, Nara, Japan

▌*Catching a Cafish with a Gourd* by Josetsu, Muromachi Period, Myoshin-ji Temple, Kyoto, Japan

▌*Wind God and Thunder God* by Tawaraya Sotatsu, Edo Period, Kyoto National Museum, Kyoto, Japan

▌*South Wind, Clear Sky (Red Fuji)* by Katsushika Hokusai, Edo Period, British Museum, London

▌*The Sea at Satta, Suruga Province* by Utagawa Hiroshige, Edo Period, British Museum, London

This page left to right: Rivera, *Flower Day*, 1925; Kahlo, *Self-Portrait with Monkey*, 1938; **Opposite page:** Rivera, *Exploitation of Mexico by Spanish Conquistadors*, 1929–45

South and Central American Art

The art of South and Central America has been characterized by a blending of Native American and European traditions. Through the eighteenth century, much Latin American art was religious in nature, as expressed in the works of the Indo-Christian and Cuzco School painters. The Mexican Muralist Movement that flourished from the 1920s to the 1960s drew inspiration from a very different faith. Mural painters such as Diego Rivera (1886–1957) and David Alfaro Siqueiros (1896–1974) expressed a revolutionary politics drawn from Marxism and the Mexican Revolution.

LIST OF WORKS

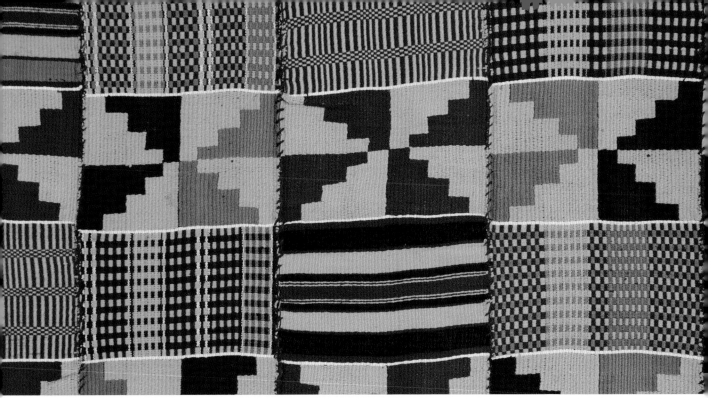

Top to bottom: Kente cloth (detail) of the Ashanti people, Ghana; bronze hyena

African Art

African art is richly diverse, reflecting the many cultures that inhabit the continent. Much traditional African art was produced to serve religious or ritual functions. In part because of this, most African art is abstract rather than representative, and humans, animals, and natural forms are depicted in highly stylized ways. Many twentieth-century Western artists were profoundly influenced by African art, which inspired them in their experimental quest for new modes of visual expression. The earliest African art can be traced to cave paintings thousands of years old. Terracotta sculptures from the Nok culture of Nigeria date back to 500 B.C.

LIST OF WORKS

- *Character Laying One's Chin on One's Knee*, Nok sculpture, Nigeria, Louvre, Paris

- *Seated Dignitary*, Nok sculpture, Nigeria, Minneapolis Institute of Arts

- Bronze ceremonial vessel, Igbo-Ukwu, Nigeria, British Museum, London

- Bronze pendant, Igbo-Ukwu, Nigeria, British Museum, London

- Bronze plaque of a warrior flanked by two shieldbearers, Benin, British Museum, London

- Bronze plaque of an oba with attendants and Europeans, Benin, British Museum, London

- Brass head of a king, Benin, Cambridge University Museum of Archaeology and Anthropology

- *Woman and Child*, Jenne sculpture, Mali, Museum of Fine Arts, Houston

- Fetish figure, Yombe sculpture, Angola, Detroit Institute of Arts

- Female figure, Bambara sculpture, Mali, National Museum of African Art, Smithsonian Institution, Washington, D.C.

- Jar, Makonde, Tanzania, National Museum of African Art, Smithsonian Institution, Washington, D.C.

- Figure, Makonde sculpture, Tanzania, National Museum of African Art, Smithsonian Institution, Washington, D.C.

- Cap mask, Yoruba, Nigeria, National Museum of African Art, Smithsonian Institution, Washington, D.C.

- Shoulder mask, Baga, Guinea, National Museum of African Art, Smithsonian Institution, Washington, D.C.

- Cloth currency bundle, Mbun, Democratic Republic of the Congo, National Museum of African Art, Smithsonian Institution, Washington, D.C.

- Mask, Tusyan, Upper Volta, Les Musées Barbier-Mueller, Geneva, Switzerland

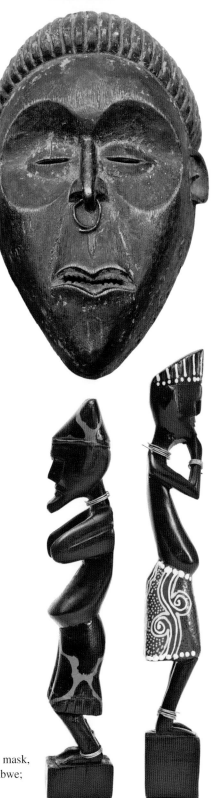

Top to bottom: Antique African mask, Ndebele tribe, Bulawayo, Zimbabwe; wooden figurines

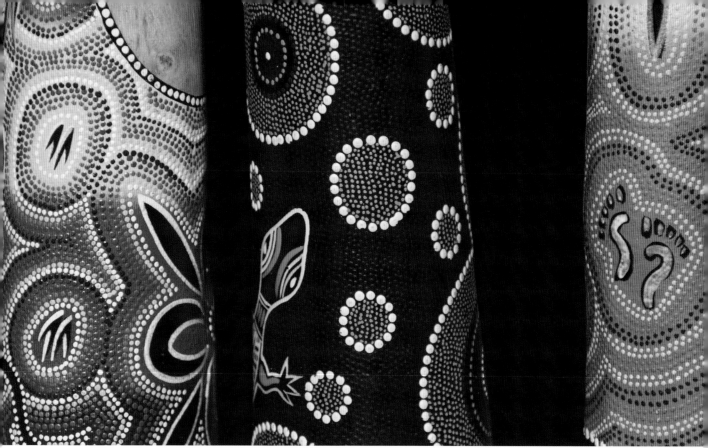

■ Didgeridoo designs

The Art of Australasia

The indigenous artistic traditions of Australia and New Zealand have retained their vitality in the modern world. The Aboriginal people of Australia preserve forms of expression that can be traced back 30,000 years. Aboriginal art is a way of connecting their people with the land and the supernatural. The Maori art of New Zealand also reflected the spiritual beliefs of this Polynesian people. Human figures are represented in a highly stylized fashion, often decorated with or surrounded by spirals symbolizing life and strength.

LIST OF WORKS

■ Aboriginal rock art, Ubirr Art Site, Kakadu National Park, Australia

■ Macassan stone arrangement, Yirrkala, Northern Territory, Australia

■ Aboriginal boomerang, National Museum of Australia, Canberra

■ Aboriginal shield, National Museum of Australia, Canberra

■ Carved head, Museum of New Zealand Te Papa, Wellington

■ Treasure box, Museum of New Zealand Te Papa, Wellington

■ Ceremonial adze, Museum of New Zealand Te Papa, Wellington

■ Pounamu pendant in human form, Museum of New Zealand Te Papa, Wellington

▌**Top:** *Kangaroo*, unknown Aboriginal artist, 1995; **Bottom:** Aboriginal rock art of the Gagudju people, Northern Australia

Chapter 2

Architecture

Sir Christopher Wren, one of the greatest architects in English history, first made a name for himself as a mathematician and astronomer. After reading some books on architecture, he wrote a treatise on building in which he related mathematical laws and artistic design. This caught the attention of King Charles II, who sent messengers to approach Wren as an architectural consultant. In 1669, Wren was appointed the King's Surveyor of Works.

Wren's greatest achievement was the rebuilding of St. Paul's Cathedral after the 1666 Great Fire of London, on which he spent thirty-six years. Wren worked on many other buildings, including the Guildhall at Windsor, which served as the town hall for that municipality. The upper-floor meeting room of the building was surrounded by colonnades that allowed for a street-level corn market.

One source relates that the town councilors were worried that the colonnades would not support the weight of the upper floor. Wren assured them that there was no problem with the structural design of the building. Despite this, the councilors insisted on additional pillars to strengthen the building. Wren, who had a wry sense of humor, built the four pillars, but deliberately left them short of the ceiling to make his point. Wren's intentions cannot be proven, but the pillars exist, decorative, but bearing no weight. The Guildhall at Windsor is an illustration of the architectural tension between artistic vision and public functionality.

Greek Architecture

Classical Greece has been an inspiration to Western architects for 2,500 years. Its echoes can be found from Thomas Jefferson's University of Virginia to many of the public buildings in Washington, D.C. This ancient architecture sought to express balance and harmony. Temples were the most distinctive form of Greek building, and were characterized by elegant rows of columns that supported the roof and opened the building to the world. These columns could be of the thicker and more massive Doric order, or of the slender and graceful Ionian order. The style of column used was carefully coordinated with the proportions of the rest of the building.

LIST OF WORKS

- Temple of Apollo, Corinth, Greece
- Temple of Aphaia, Aegina, Greece
- Temple of Apollo Epikourios ("Apollo the Helper"), Bassae, Greece
- Temple of Poseidon, Sounion, Greece
- Erechtheion, Athens, Greece
- Tholos of Athena, Delphi, Greece
- Temple of Hera, Paestum, Italy
- Temple of Athena, Paestum, Italy
- Temple of Poseidon, Paestum, Italy
- Temple of Concord, Agrigento, Sicily
- Greek Temple from Xanthos, British Museum, London
- Pergamon Altar, Pergamon Museum, Berlin, Germany
- Theater of Dionysus, Athens, Greece
- Theater of Asklepios, Epidaurus, Greece

The Parthenon, Athens

■ Sanctuary of Apollo
  at Delphi

■ Temple of Hephaestus

Roman Architecture

The Romans were heavily influenced by Greek architecture, and many Roman temples show the mix of Greek and more traditional Roman building styles. But the Romans went far beyond the Greeks in their use of the arch, the vault, and the dome. This and the innovative use of brick and concrete enabled the Romans to construct buildings on a vaster scale than the Greeks. The Colosseum could seat 50,000 people. The dome of the Pantheon, still the largest unreinforced concrete dome in the world, gave the building a sense of vertiginous spaciousness unlike anything in Greek architecture.

❚**Top to bottom, left to right:** Basilica of Maxentius; Bath at Caracalla; Basilica of Maxentius (detail)

■ **Top to bottom:** Pantheon, Rome; ceiling detail; Colosseum, Rome; archway detail

▌Ponte du Garde, Nîmes, France

Public Works to Serve the People

The Romans were masterful engineers as well as architects. Roman public works allowed people to enjoy a level of physical comfort that would not be seen again for a thousand years. Roman roads were built so well that some are still in use today. Roman aqueducts supplied cities with running water. The city of Rome was serviced by eleven aqueducts, bringing water from as far as fifty-nine miles away. Hadrian's Wall, a defensive structure that protected Roman Britain from barbarians to the north, ran for seventy-three miles.

PLACES OF NOTE

- Roman Forum, Rome
- Circus Maximus, Rome
- Arch of Titus, Rome
- Arch of Constantine, Rome
- Baths of Diocletian, Rome
- Trajan's Column, Rome
- Pompeii, Italy

- Insula, Ostia, Italy
- Tower of Hercules, A Coruña, Spain
- Aqueduct of Segovia, Segovia, Spain
- Maison Carrée, Nîmes, France
- Amphitheatre, El Djem, Tunisia
- Porta Nigra, Trier, Germany
- Diocletian's Palace, Split, Croatia

Hadrian's Wall, northern Britain

Basilicas and Cathedrals

Basilicas in ancient Rome were dedicated to public business. Once the Emperor Constantine issued his Edict of Toleration for Christians in A.D. 313, basilicas became the preferred model for large Christian churches. Most contained a central nave, with aisles on either side. On one end there would be a raised apse where the altar was placed. Perhaps the greatest basilica in the western world is St. Peter's Basilica. Built in the sixteenth and early seventeenth century, it was contributed to by many great Renaissance artists, including Raphael, Michelangelo, and Bernini. St. Peter's Basilica has the most spacious interior of any church in Europe.

LIST OF WORKS

- Basilica of Constantine, Trier, Germany
- Hagia Sophia, Istanbul, Turkey
- Basilica of San Vitale, Ravenna, Italy
- Church of the Nativity, Bethlehem
- Aachen Cathedral, Aachen, Germany
- Basilica of St. John Lateran, Vatican City, Rome
- Basilica of St. Paul Outside the Walls, Rome
- Basilica of Our Lady of Guadalupe, Mexico City
- Basilica of the Shrine of the Immaculate Conception, Washington, D.C.
- Basilica di Sana Maria del Fiore, Florence, Italy
- Basilica di Santa Maria del Fiore, Florence, Italy

■ St. Peter's Basilica, Vatican City

Left to right: St. Paul's Cathedral, London; Westminster Abbey, London; Domes of St. Mark's Cathedral, Venice; St. Martin's in the Field, London

Churches and Cathedrals

In the eleventh and twelfth centuries the Romanesque style of architecture spread through Europe and reshaped the construction of churches. Romanesque builders modified the original Roman basilica plan by replacing wooden roofs with stone barrel vaults. Some experimented further by crossing two barrel vaults in a cruciform shape. To bear the added weight of the stone vaults, Romanesque churches had thick pillars and walls, with narrow windows. In the twelfth and thirteenth centuries, Romanesque gave way to Gothic architecture. The introduction of ribbed and pointed vaults allowed the interior spaces of Gothic cathedrals to soar to dizzying heights. The innovation of flying buttresses—stone arches built onto the outsides of a structure—helped bear the immense weight of the vault. This made possible thinner walls and the creation of large and elaborate stained-glass windows, which bathed the interior of Gothic cathedrals with sacred light. The great Gothic cathedrals brilliantly blended the engineering skill and intense religiosity of medieval Europe.

PLACES OF INTEREST

▌Angouleme Cathedral, Angouleme, France

▌Speyer Cathedral, Speyer, Germany

▌Sainte-Chapelle, Paris, France

▌Cathedral of Our Lady of Chartres, Chartres, France

▌Cathedral of Notre Dame of Reims, Reims, France

▌Notre Dame Cathedral, Paris

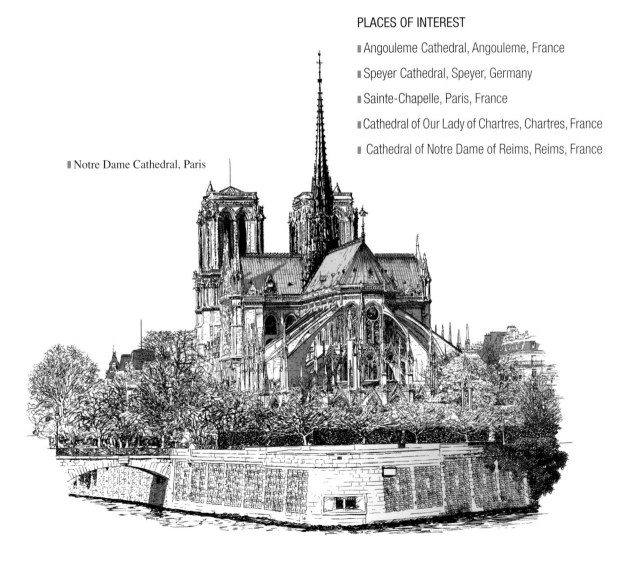

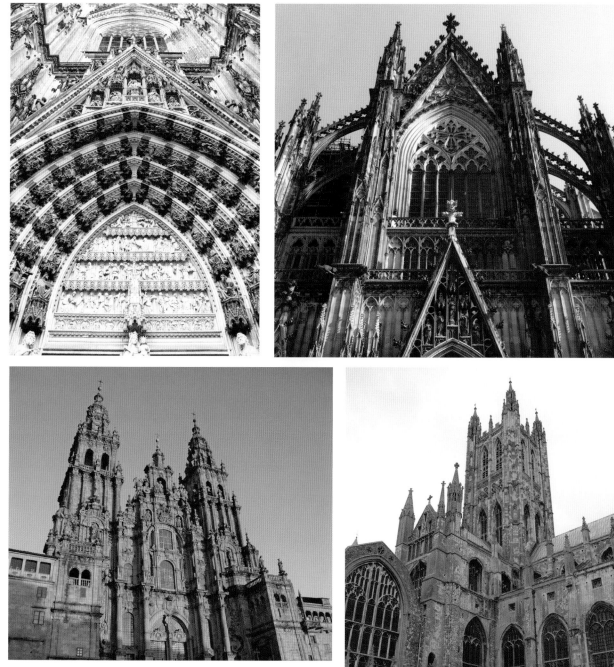

▌**Clockwise from top left:** Detail of the façade of Cologne Cathedral, Cologne, Germany; Cologne Cathedral; Canterbury Cathedral, Canterbury, England; Santiago de Compostela, Galicia, Spain

St. Basil's Cathedral, Moscow

Cathedrals and Churches

Great churches have arisen outside Western Europe. Influenced by Constantinople and the Byzantine Empire, Russian Orthodox Church architecture is distinguished by its bright colors and onion-shaped domes. But in Russia, Byzantine churches flowered into multidomed structures that placed a greater emphasis on verticality in their lines. In the United States, many congregations emulated European models in their churches. In the nineteenth and early twentieth centuries, Gothic Revival architecture flourished, both in churches and elsewhere. St. Patrick's Cathedral, constructed between 1858 and 1878, is the seat of the Roman Catholic Archdiocese of New York. The cathedral is so large that it takes up a whole city block. Building began on the Episcopal Cathedral of St. John the Divine, also in New York, in 1892 and remains unfinished. The Episcopal Washington National Cathedral construction began in 1907, and its last stone was laid in 1990.

PLACES OF INTEREST

- St. Sophia Cathedral, Novgorod, Russia
- Church of Archangel Gabriel (Menshikov Tower), Moscow
- St. Patrick's Cathedral, New York
- Trinity Church, New York
- Washington National Cathedral, Washington, D.C.

■ Details of the Cathedral of St. John the Divine, New York City

Skyscrapers

The first modern skyscrapers rose in the United States during the late nineteenth century. They received their name for their then-towering height of ten stories or more. Skyscrapers were made possible by new construction methods using steel frames that allowed buildings to soar past the load-bearing capacity of masonry. The new skyscrapers allowed the maximal use of scarce and increasingly valuable real estate in America's booming cities. Architects such as Daniel Burnham and the visionary Louis Sullivan pioneered the design and construction of these buildings. Sullivan celebrated the new architectural grammar that came with high-rise buildings, dismissing the concerns of critics still rooted in classicism; he famously declared that "form ever follows function." By the 1930s, skyscrapers such as the legendary Empire State Building in New York City had given American cities their distinctive skylines. Skyscrapers soon spread around the world, and by the early twenty-first century the tallest buildings were located outside the United States.

PLACES OF INTEREST

- Wainwright Building, St. Louis, Missouri
- Flatiron Building, New York
- Woolworth Building, New York
- Chrysler Building, New York
- Petronas Twin Towers, Kuala Lumpur, Malaysia
- International Commerce Centre, West Kowloon, Hong Kong

▍**Clockwise from left:** Shanghai World Financial Center, Shanghai, China; Burj Khalifa, Dubai, United Arab Emirates; Taipei 101, Taipei, China; Willis Tower (formerly Sears Tower), Chicago

Bridges

In the nineteenth century the same revolution in methods and materials that made skyscrapers possible led to an explosion in the length of bridges. Suspension bridges making use of chains had been built in Tibet as early as the fifteenth century. The first modern suspension bridge using chains was erected over Jacob's Creek in Westmoreland County, Pennsylvania, in 1801. Fifteen years later, wire-cable bridges began to appear. The greatest of the nineteenth-century bridge builders was John Augustus Roebling, a German immigrant to the United States, who literally carried wire-cable suspension bridges to new heights. Roebling had already constructed the longest suspension bridge in the world at Cincinnati, Ohio, when he was commissioned to span the East River in New York City. Roebling designed the Brooklyn Bridge, the first steel-cable suspension bridge, but died as a result of an accident during construction. His son, Washington Augustus Roebling, supervised the completion of his father's greatest work.

PLACES OF INTEREST

- John A. Roebling Suspension Bridge, Cincinnati, Ohio, and Covington, Kentucky

- Mackinac Bridge, Straits of Mackinac, Michigan

- Verrazano-Narrows Bridge, Staten Island and Brooklyn, New York

- Akashi Kaikyo Bridge, Awaji Island and Kobe, Japan

- Xihoumen Bridge, Jintang Island and Cezi Island, China

Clockwise from top left: Sio-Se Pol Bridge on the Zayandeh River, Isfahan, Iran; Brooklyn Bridge, New York City; Chapel Bridge, Lucerne, Switzerland; Sydney Harbor Bridge, Sydney, Australia; Firth of Forth Rail Bridge, Scotland

Castles and Palaces

Since the dawn of civilization, rulers have built imposing residences for themselves. At Mycenae in pre-Classical Greece and at Knossos in Crete, palaces were probably administrative and economic centers as well as royal residences. The pharaohs of Egypt and the Great Kings of Persia built palatial complexes for themselves, designed to impress as well as intimidate. The Roman emperor Nero went too far in his efforts to celebrate his reign when he built a lavishly decorated pleasure palace in the heart of Rome on land cleared by the great fire of 64. Known as the Domus Aurea ("Golden House") because of all the gold leaf used in its construction, its excess probably contributed to Nero's overthrow in 68. In the seventeenth century, King Louis XIV of France built a showcase palace at Versailles, outside Paris. Not only did the Palace of Versailles display the Sun King's power, but its spaciousness also allowed him to keep an eye on his fractious nobility.

PLACES OF INTEREST

▌Palace of Minos, Heraklion, Crete, Greece

▌Imperial Palace, Tokyo, Japan

▌Windsor Castle, Windsor, England

▌Peterhof Palace, St. Petersburg, Russia

▌Schönbrunn Palace, Vienna, Austria

▌ The Forbidden City, Beijing, China

id="4" /> Alhambra Palace, Granada, Spain   ▌ Alcázar, Seville, Spain

▌ Palace of Versailles, Versailles, France

Fortresses

Given humanity's propensity for violent conflict, enormous ingenuity and effort have been expended on fortifications. The remains of prehistoric hill forts and ring forts can be found across Europe. With the advent of civilization, cities built walls for their defense. The walls of ancient Babylon were famous, while those guarding Athens and its port at Piraeus gave the city the security to take the leading place in Classical Greece. The growing sophistication of fortifications required commensurate skills to overcome these defenses. Demetrius I of Macedon received the title "The Besieger" because of his talent for taking cities. The unsettled conditions of the Middle Ages encouraged fortifications. Initially, castles were made of wood and earth, but by the eleventh century they increasingly were built of stone. Castles dominated European warfare until the advent of gunpowder. Artillery did not end fortification. Engineers such as Louis XIV's Marquis de Vauban designed star-shaped forts with lower, thicker walls that were relatively impervious to cannon fire.

PLACES OF INTEREST

- Lion's Gate, Mycenae, Greece

- Aurelian Wall, Rome

- Tower of London, London

- Krak des Chevaliers, Homs Governorate, Syria

- Citadel of Besançon, Besançon, France

- **Clockwise from top right:** Tiled walls and ceiling of Topkapi Palace, Istanbul, Turkey; images of Raphael's Loggias in the Winter Palace, St. Petersburg, Russia; tower in the Castillo de San Marcos fort, St. Augustine, Florida; Buckingham Palace, London; detail of the Alamo, San Antonio, Texas

Homes and Halls:
The Home as Refuge

That a man's home is his castle has been taken literally in the past. Some of the great English country homes were once fortified dwellings, offering their residents security in troubled times. Peace made many homes refuges of a different sort. They became places to escape public burdens and to renew private spirits. In 1783, the ill-fated Queen Marie-Antoinette of France ordered the construction of the Hamlet at Versailles. This was a reproduction of a French peasant village, complete with cracked and weathered timbers. Here she attempted to escape the rigid formality of the nearby court. Catherine the Great, Empress of Russia, also wanted a rural getaway. Deciding that she did not like the first version of Tsaritsyno, she had it torn down, and she died before the second was completed. During long years of public service, George Washington and Thomas Jefferson yearned for their beloved homes at Mount Vernon and Monticello, respectively.

‖ Gardens at Sandringham House, Norfolk, England

PLACES OF INTEREST

■ Lake Palace Hotel, Udaipur, India

■ Tai Fu Tai, Hong Kong

■ The Queen's Hamlet, Versailles, France

■ Tsaritsyno, Moscow

■ Mount Vernon, Alexandria, Virginia

■ **Clockwise from top left:** Castle Howard, Yorkshire, England; detail of a fountain at Castle Howard; House of the Seven Gables, Salem, Massachusetts; Monticello, Charlottesville, Virginia

Homes and Halls:
The Home as Showpiece

Homes can be showpieces as well as residences. Blenheim Palace was given to the Duke of Marlborough as a reward for his military services in the War of the Spanish Succession. This massive palace was the birthplace of Marlborough's descendant Winston Churchill. In the late nineteenth century, many American industrialists built homes that reflected their wealth and power. George Washington Vanderbilt II, an heir to the Vanderbilt family fortune, constructed Biltmore House in North Carolina, modeled on a French château. Biltmore House remains the largest private residence in the United States. The newspaper magnate William Randolph Hearst built a huge California home that reflected its owner's eclectic architectural tastes. Hearst filled the place with his purchases from around the world, including the façade of a Greek temple. Orson Welles satirized Hearst Castle as "Xanadu" in his muckraking film *Citizen Kane* (1941). Frank Lloyd Wright's Taliesin estate in Spring Green, Wisconsin, was simultaneously a home and an advertisement for his innovative architectural principles.

▌Fallingwater, Fayette County, Pennsylvania

PLACES OF INTEREST

- Blenheim Palace, Woodstock, Oxfordshire, England
- Biltmore House, Asheville, North Carolina
- Taliesin Estate, Spring Green, Wisconsin
- Hearst Castle, San Simeon, California
- Bill Gates's House (Xanadu 2.0), Medina, Washington
- Otahuna Lodge, near Christchurch, New Zealand

Top to bottom: The Breakers, Newport, Rhode Island, CC-BY-SA-3.0/Matt H. Wade at Wikipedia; Miramare Castle, Trieste, Italy

Chapter 3

Wonders

The Athenian Phidias was the greatest sculptor of his day, and a creator of the Classical style that became a foundation of Western art. He was an associate of the Athenian leader Pericles, and as superintendent of public works he oversaw the building of the Parthenon. Phidias carved the great statue of the goddess Athena that stood at the heart of the temple. This statue was chryselephantine, meaning that it was made of ivory and gold, with much of Athena's clothing being sheets of gold.

Political enemies of Pericles prosecuted Phidias on various charges, forcing him to leave Athens. This led to his greatest commission. A new temple of Zeus had been erected at Olympia, and the caretakers invited Phidias to sculpt a massive statue of the god for the temple. Archaeological investigation has found remains of the workshop behind the temple, as well as a cup with the inscription "I belong to Phidias."

The enormous chryselephantine statue of Zeus that Phidias fashioned became one of the wonders of the ancient world. It was unusual because it depicted Zeus majestically seated on a throne instead of hurling a thunderbolt. Phidias claimed that his inspiration for the statue came from some lines of Homer. When he was finished, Phidias carved his signature at the foot of the statue and prayed that the god would send him a sign if Zeus was satisfied with the work. Immediately, lightning rent the sky, signaling Zeus's approval. Phidias's statue is gone now, but many wonders remain in the world.

Remarkable Museums

The artistic heritage of Western civilization is richly represented in the magnificent museums that have sprung up in the great cities of Europe and America. Some, like the Guggenheim Museum in New York City, were endowed by private benefactors. Others, like the Louvre in Paris, are maintained by national governments. All ensure that everyone can enjoy great art.

▌Opposite page clockwise from left:
Guggenheim museum in New York City;
The State Hermitage Museum at night in
St.Petersburg, Russia; Museo del Prado,
Madrid, Spain; Louvre Museum Courtyard
at night, Paris, France; **This page:** The
British Museum, London

PLACES OF INTEREST

▌Metropolitan Museum of Art, New York City

▌Vatican Museums, Vatican City, Rome

▌Uffizi Gallery of Florence, Florence, Italy

▌J. Paul Getty Center, Los Angeles

▌Musée d'Orsay, Paris

▌National Gallery of Art, Washington, D.C.

▌Museum of Modern Art, New York City

▌Art Institute of Chicago

Places of Worship around the World

The human quest for the transcendent has found many expressions. While Christians were building cathedrals, Native Americans, Hindus, and Buddhists were also erecting spectacular monuments to their piety. In North America, the Mound Builders left behind mysterious earthen reminders of their lost civilization. In Central and South America, the Maya, Aztecs, and Inca created massive stone temples for their deities. Hinduism can be traced back thousands of years in Indian history. The rich variety of Hindu traditions has led to a wide array of temples and religious sites. Buddhism originated in India, but then spread throughout Asia, resulting in many different national styles of temples.

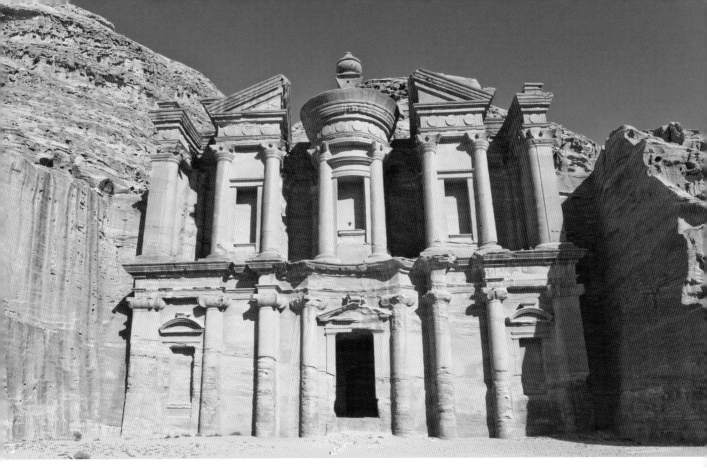

▌**Clockwise from left:** Golden roof of the Jokhang Temple, Tibet; Potala Palace in Lhasa, Tibet; Angkor Wat at sunset, Cambodia; the façade of the monastery Al Khazneh; Borobudur, a Mahayana Buddhist temple in Central Java, Indonesia, from the ninth century with a main shrine and several perforated stupas

Places of Worship around the World

- Monk's Mound, Cahokia Mounds State Historic Site, Collinsville, Illinois
- Grave Creek Mound, Moundsville, West Virginia
- Templo Mayor, Mexico City
- Santa Cecilia Acatitlán, Mexico State, Mexico
- Temple of the Feathered Serpent, Xochicalco, Municipality of Miacatlán, Morelos State, Mexico
- Pyramid of the Sun, Teotihuacán, San Juan Teotihuacán Municipality, Mexico State, Mexico
- The Castle, Chichen Itza, Yucatan State, Mexico
- Temple of the Cross, Palenque, Chiapas State, Mexico

- Temple of the Moon, Huayna Picchu, Peru
- The Golden Temple, Amritsar, India
- Sri Ranganathaswamy Temple, Srirangam, India
- Brihadeeswarar Temple, Thanjavur, India
- Nallur Kandaswamy Temple, Nallur, Sri Lanka
- Tiger's Nest Monastery, Paro Valley, Bhutan
- Wat Rong Khun, Chiang Rai, Thailand
- Shwedagon Pagoda, Yangon, Myanmar
- Chion-in Temple, Kyoto, Japan
- Temple of Heaven, Beijing, China

Clockwise from top left: Wat Arun (Temple of the Dawn), Bangkok, Thailand; Pha That Luang, Vientiane, Laos; Tikal, El Petén, Guatamala; Ancient Buddhist temple, Bagan, Myanmar; Praying under rain at the Wailing Wall, Jerusalem

▌**Opposite page:** Spirit Way at the Ming Dynasty Tombs, Beijing; **This page left to right:** Tomb of Tutankhamun at Valley of the Kings near Luxor, Egypt; a view of the Taj Mahal in Agra, India

Tombs
and Tributes

From the dawn of civilization, great rulers have sought to ensure their people's memory of them through great tombs. Sometimes their people have desired the same thing. The Great Pyramid of Giza was the final resting place for the Egyptian Pharaoh Khufu. Few leaders could match the size of Khufu's monument, but many have compensated for this through the magnificence and ornamentation of their burial places. The Mughal Emperor Shah Jahan built the Taj Mahal for his beloved third wife, and in time he joined her there.

PLACES OF INTEREST

▌Great Pyramid of Khufu, Giza, Egypt

▌Tomb of Cyrus the Great, Pasargadae World Heritage Site, Iran

▌Tomb of Philip II of Macedon, Vergina, Greece

▌Hadrian's Tomb (Castel Sant'Angelo), Rome

▌Mosque of the Prophet, Medina, Saudi Arabia

▌St. Peter's Basilica, Vatican City, Rome

▌Westminster Abbey, London

▌Napoleon's Tomb, Les Invalides, Paris

▌General Grant National Memorial, New York City

▌Lenin's Tomb, Moscow

Temples and Synagogues

The first Jewish temple was built in Jerusalem by King Solomon in the tenth century B.C. It was destroyed by the Babylonians in 586 B.C. In 515 B.C. the Jews dedicated a second temple, begun when they returned from captivity in Babylon. Herod the Great reconstructed the temple around 20 B.C., but that temple was destroyed by the Romans in A.D. 70, as they crushed a Jewish rebellion. Only the Wailing Wall remains. Today, Jews worship in synagogues around the world.

PLACES OF INTEREST

▍Portuguese Synagogue, Amsterdam, Netherlands

▍Jews' Court, Lincoln, England

▍Touro Synagogue, Newport, Rhode Island

▍Kahal Zur Israel Synagogue, Recife, Brazil

▍Bialystoker Synogogue, New York City

▍Grand Choral Synagogue, St. Petersburg, Russia

▍Great Synagogue of Rome, Rome

▍Abuhav Synagogue, Safed, Israel

▍Temple Emanu-El, New York City

▍**Opposite page:** Budapest Great Synagogue; **This page top to bottom:** The Mormon Church's Temple Square in Salt Lake City, Utah; Great Synagogue of Florence, Italy

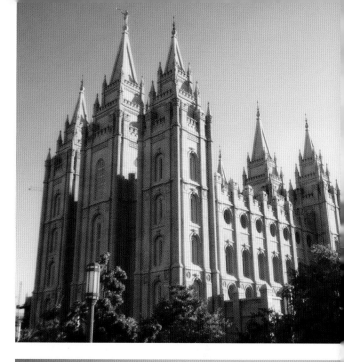

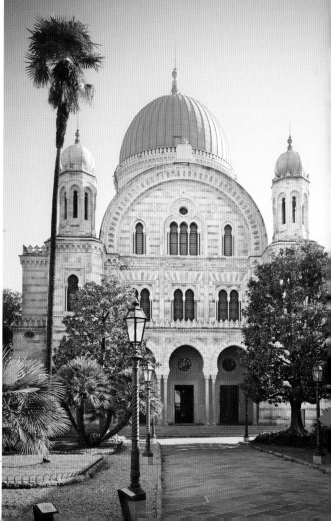

Mosques

In the very earliest days of Islam, Muslims prayed in the open. Soon, however, they began building distinctive houses of worship, and they continued to do so as they burst out of the Arabian Peninsula into the wider world. Today, across the globe mosques offer Muslims a place to pray and to further their education in their faith. *Imams* lead their congregations in prayer and preach sermons on Friday. Mosques are also important social centers, especially for Muslims living in the Western world. Mosques collect and distribute Muslim charitable contributions and also provide a place for conflict resolution within the community.

Left to right: Worshipers performing Tawaf (circumambulating) the Kaaba, the most sacred site in Islam; this picture was taken from the gate of Abdul Aziz. Interior of Shat Gombuj Mosque in Bagerhat, Bangladesh; **Opposite page:** Selimiye Mosque, Edirne, Turkey

Domes and Minarets

Most mosques are architecturally distinctive. Many feature tall minarets, from which the faithful are called to prayer. Since the days of the Ottoman Turks, large central domes have been a common feature, often combined with smaller domes covering other wings of the building. All mosques have a prayer hall, oriented so worshipers can pray in the direction of Mecca.

PLACES OF INTEREST

- The Holy Mosque, Mecca, Saudi Arabia
- Quba Mosque, Medina, Saudi Arabia
- The Mosque of Uqba, Kairouan, Tunisia
- Umayyad Mosque, Damascus, Syria
- Tekkiye Mosque, Damascus, Syria
- Great Mosque of Aleppo, Aleppo, Syria
- Imam Ali Mosque, Najaf, Iraq

- Ibn Tulun Mosque, Cairo, Egypt
- Al-Azhar Mosque, Cairo, Egypt
- Royal Mosque, Lahore, Pakistan
- Beyazit Mosque, Istanbul, Turkey
- Imam Mosque, Isfahan, Iran
- Great Mosque of Xi'an, Xi'an, China
- Baitul Futuh Mosque, London
- Istiqlal Mosque, Jakarta, Indonesia

This page top to bottom: Imam Reza Shrine, Mashhad, Iran; Dome of the Rock on the Temple Mount, Jerusalem, Israel; **Opposite page:** Blue Mosque, Istanbul, Turkey

Landmarks

People invest some places with special significance. These landmarks can be manmade, or they can be sites of natural beauty and power. What these special places all have in common is that they speak to those who see them, conveying a meaning that goes beyond the obvious. The Statue of Liberty became a beacon of freedom to generations of immigrants arriving in the United States. The Eiffel Tower embodied the technological daring and cultural confidence of late nineteenth-century Europe. Mount Fuji, famous for its size and symmetrical shape, was long regarded as a sacred place and over time became a symbol of Japan.

PLACES OF INTEREST

- Mount Rushmore National Memorial, Keystone, South Dakota

- Niagara Falls, Niagara Falls, Ontario and New York

- Lincoln Memorial, Washington, D.C.

- Gateway Arch, St. Louis, Missouri

- Alamo Mission, San Antonio, Texas

- Angel Falls, Bolívar State, Venezuela

- Christ on the Corcovado, Rio de Janeiro, Brazil

- Machu Picchu, Cuzco region, Peru

- Sphinx, Giza, Egypt

- Victoria Falls, Livingstone, Zambia, and Victoria Falls, Zimbabwe

- Mount Kilimanjaro, Kilimanjaro National Park, Tanzania

- Tower of London, London

- Big Ben, London

- Arc de Triomphe, Paris

- Sydney Opera House, Sydney, Australia

- Great Barrier Reef, Australia

- Great Buddha of Kamakura, Kamakura, Japan

- Mount Everest, Nepal

- Mount Fuji, Japan

Opposite page top to bottom: Brandenburg Gate, Berlin, Germany; Statue of Liberty with New York City backdrop; Grand Canyon afterglow; **This page:** Eiffel Tower, Paris, France

Buildings of State

Many buildings become identified with the governmental bodies that they house. The White House in the United States, 10 Downing Street in the United Kingdom, and the Kremlin in Russia have all become synonymous with executive power in these nations. The elevation of buildings into symbols reflects a political continuity that transcends the coming and going of individual leaders.

PLACES OF INTEREST

- Capitol Hill, Washington, D.C.
- Los Pinos, Mexico City
- Buckingham Palace, London
- Westminster Palace, London
- Élysée Palace, Paris
- Vatican Palace, Vatican City, Rome
- Great Hall of the People, Beijing
- Kantei, official residence of Japan's prime minister, Tokyo

Opposite page top to bottom: German parliament building—the Reichstag—illuminated at night, Berlin, Germany; the Kremlin from Kamenny Bridge, Moscow; **This page top to bottom:** The White House, Washington, D.C.; 10 Downing Street, home of the British prime minister

Seven Wonders of the Ancient World

Many ancient Greeks traveled through the Mediterranean, visiting what were already regarded as the wonders of their world. Lists were made of these wonders and by the second and first centuries B.C., the Seven Wonders of the World we now know had already become standard. Ironically, the oldest of the ancient wonders is the only one that survives today. The Great Pyramid of Giza was built by the Pharaoh Khufu and finished around 2560 B.C. In antiquity, a casing of glittering white limestone blocks still covered the pyramid. The Hanging Gardens of Babylon were a triumph of urban horticulture before they reportedly were destroyed by an earthquake. Around 432 B.C., the sculptor Phidias created the statue of Zeus in the god's temple at Olympia. The seated figure was made of ivory and gold-plated bronze, and towered forty-three feet from its base.

▌**Opposite page:** Great Pyramid of Giza in Egypt; **This page top to bottom:** Hanging Gardens of Babylon, depicted in a sixteenth-century engraving by Dutch artist Martin Heemskerck; Olympian Zeus (Barclay)

Seven Wonders of the Mediterranean World

The Temple of Artemis at Ephesus was financed by Croesus, the legendarily rich ruler of Lydia. The temple was the first constructed entirely of marble. A young man named Herostratus, wishing his name to be remembered, set a fire that destroyed the temple in 356 B.C. The Mausoleum of Halicarnassus, a tomb made for King Mausolus around 353 B.C., was famous for its beauty. The Colossus of Rhodes was a bronze statue of Helios erected between 292 and 280 B.C. The Colossus stood 107 feet tall, but toppled during an earthquake in 226 B.C., though its fragments remained a tourist attraction for centuries. The Lighthouse of Alexandria, built in the third century B.C., was one of the tallest edifices in the Mediterranean world. Sadly, it eventually succumbed to earthquakes during the Middle Ages.

THE TEMPLE OF ARTEMIS, EPHESUS, AS RESTORED.

❚ **Opposite page top to bottom:** The Colossus of Rhodes, depicted in this hand-colored engraving by Martin Heemskerck; Mausoleum of Halicarnassus ruins; **This page top to bottom:** Ishtar Gate detail, Babylon; Temple of Artemis, Ephesus, Turkey

Seven Wonders of the Classical and Ancient Worlds

The Colosseum is an enduring monument to the technical and aesthetic genius of ancient Rome. Completed in 80 B.C. and seating 50,000 people, the Colosseum offered a venue for "games" that included gladiatorial combats and animal hunts. Christians sometimes involuntarily provided the entertainment at the Colosseum. The Catacombs of Rome served as an underground refuge for Christians escaping persecution. However, the primary purpose of the Catacombs was as a burial site. Between the second and fourth centuries A.D., thousands of Christians were buried in the Catacombs. In China, walls to keep out invaders were constructed as far back as the seventh century B.C. The first emperor, Qin Shi Huang, built the Great Wall at enormous human cost between 220 and 206 B.C. as a protection against roving hordes of barbarians. The current Great Wall dates to the fourteenth century Ming Dynasty and runs for 3,889 miles.

Opposite page: The Great Wall of China, Jinshanling section; **This page:** The Colosseum of Rome

Seven Wonders of the Medieval World

Stonehenge was constructed sometime between 3000 and 2000 B.C. Speculation on the purpose of this prehistoric monument has a long pedigree. In the Middle Ages, Geoffrey of Monmouth wrote that Stonehenge had been created by the magician Merlin. There is no such mystery about the Hagia Sophia, erected in Constantinople in A.D. 532–537. The Emperor Justinian wanted his Church of Holy Wisdom to glorify his reign. With its great dome and enormous size, Hagia Sophia is the masterpiece of Byzantine architecture. The Leaning Tower of Pisa is the freestanding bell tower of the city's cathedral in Pisa, Italy. The tower started to lean soon after construction began in the 1170s. It has been defying gravity ever since. The Porcelain Tower of Nanjing was built in China in the fifteenth century. The brilliantly colored tower was destroyed by Taiping rebels in 1856.

❚ **This page left to right:** Leaning Tower of Pisa, Pisa, Italy; The Porcelain Tower, Nanjing, China; **Opposite page top to bottom:** The Hagia Sofia, Istanbul, Turkey; Stonehenge, Wiltshire, England

Seven Wonders of the Modern World

The Empire State Building is a beloved landmark in New York City. Constructed in 1930–1931 during the Great Depression, it symbolized New York's economic and cultural ambition. For forty years it was the tallest building in the world. The Empire State Building's iconic status was cemented by its use as the site of the climactic battle in the movie *King Kong* (1932). The CN Tower in Toronto, Ontario, Canada, is the tallest manmade structure in the Western Hemisphere. Since its opening in 1976, this communications and observation tower has become an emblem of Canadian pride. The Channel Tunnel runs under the English Channel, connecting the United Kingdom with France. Since the tunnel's completion in 1994, trains carry passengers and freight on tracks that run for more than thirty-one miles.

This page top to bottom: Train entering Channel Tunnel; scenic view of CN Tower and Toronto city waterfront skyline; **Opposite page:** Empire State Building in New York City

Seven Wonders of the Modern World

President Theodore Roosevelt championed the construction of the Panama Canal, connecting the Atlantic and Pacific oceans. Work on the canal began in 1904 and was completed in 1914. An engineering masterpiece, the Panama Canal is fifty-one miles long. The Golden Gate Bridge crosses the opening of San Francisco Bay. Built between 1933 and 1937, its main span was once the longest in the world. It is still one of the world's most beautiful bridges. The Itaipu Dam is the globe's largest hydroelectric plant. It opened in 1984 and is located on the Paraná River, which separates Brazil from Paraguay. The Deltaworks is a complex system of dams, channels, and water engineering works designed to control flooding in the Rhine-Meuse-Scheldt delta of the Netherlands. Construction began in 1950 and continues to this day.

Opposite page: Golden Gate Bridge, San Francisco, California; **This page top to bottom:** Gutan Locks at the Panama Canal; the Oosterscheldedam, part of the Dutch Deltaworks in the Netherlands; the Itaipu Dam on the Paraná River, which forms the border between Brazil and Paraguay

Chapter 4

Music and Composers

Wolfgang Amadeus Mozart was so musically gifted that he began performing and composing as a young child. His father Leopold, a great musician himself, took the prodigy on tour across Europe. When Mozart was fourteen, he and his father attended a Holy Week performance of Gregorio Allegri's *Miserere* at the Papal Chapel in Rome. The *Miserere* was a notoriously difficult piece, and the papal choir had allowed only a few copies of the score to be made, jealously guarding one of their signature pieces. That night Mozart wrote down the music from memory. A few days later he performed the piece in front of an audience that included the celebrated singer Christofori, a member of the papal choir. The result was a musical sensation that added to Mozart's fame. It was generally conceded that no musical secrets could be kept from the young genius.

Mozart showed no more respect for authority years later, by which time he had become a celebrated composer. His opera *The Abduction from the Seraglio* was commissioned by the Austrian emperor Joseph II, and premiered in Vienna on July 16, 1782. Emperor Joseph II, a highly intelligent man with a keen appreciation of music, shared the common contemporary criticism that Mozart's work was too complex. After the performance, he approached Mozart and said, "That is too fine for my ears—there are too many notes." To which Mozart replied, "There are just as many notes as there should be." As with Mozart, music follows its own laws.

The Emergence of Medieval Music

During the Middle Ages, the foundations of modern music took shape, and the systems of notes and scales began to emerge. Early in the period, plainsong dominated liturgical music, the most famous version of this being Gregorian chant. In the twelfth century, composers experimented with an early version of polyphony, adding one voice and then more, achieving new effects in harmony. By the end of the period, religious and secular music was becoming more rhythmically complex.

PEOPLE OF NOTE

- Hildegard of Bingen (1098–1179)
- Bernart de Ventadorn (ca. 1135–ca. 1195)
- Gautier de Coincy (1177–1236)
- Pérotin (fl. ca. 1200)
- Adam de la Halle (ca. 1237–ca. 1288)
- Franco of Cologne (fl. ca. 1250)
- Philippe de Vitry (1291–1361)
- Guillaume de Machaut (1300–1377)
- Francesco Landini (ca. 1330–1397)
- Johannes Ciconia (ca. 1370–1412)
- Leonel Power (ca. 1380–1445)
- John Dunstaple (ca. 1390–1453)

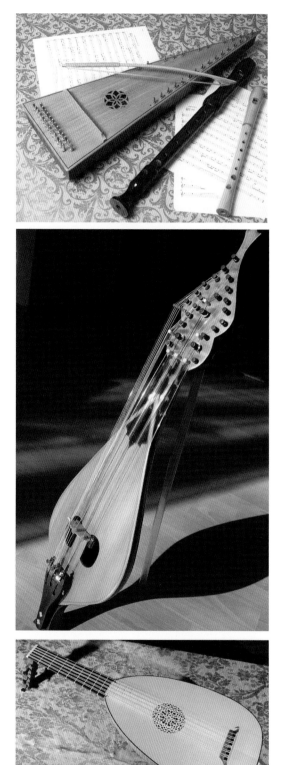

Clockwise from top right: An ensemble of bowed psaltery with alto and soprano recorders resting on sheet music; fifteenth-century sackbut; lute; mountain dulcimer

Music in the Renaissance

During the Renaissance, with its increasingly sophisticated approach to the arts, polyphony flourished. New instruments appeared, such as the viol and the harpsichord, which profoundly influenced the future of music. Musical works were more dramatically expressive, and composers increasingly became known for their distinctive styles. Instrumental ensembles grew in size, allowing for richer sounds and more complicated textures, setting the stage for orchestral music.

❚ **This page top to bottom:** Vintage lithograph depicting a fourteenth-century scene of a group of Italian women socializing; tambourine; *Ricercar del Sesto Tuono* by Gabrieli; **Opposite page top to bottom:** Seventeenth-century violin decorated with spiral scroll work and the royal arms of the Stuarts; three German musicians playing a lute, harp, and slide trombone; stone carving of an angel playing a shawm pipe

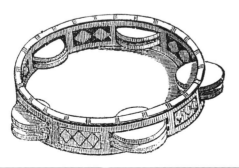

PEOPLE OF NOTE

- Guillaume Dufay (ca. 1397–1474)
- Johannes Ockeghem (ca. 1420–1497)
- Josquin des Prez (ca. 1450–1521)
- Antoine Brumel (ca. 1460–ca. 1513)
- John Taverner (ca. 1490–1545)
- Nicolas Gombert (ca. 1495–ca. 1560)
- Cipriano de Rore (ca. 1515–1565)
- Giovanni Pierluigi da Palestrina (ca. 1525–1594)
- Orlande de Lassus (ca. 1532–1594)
- William Byrd (ca. 1540–1623)
- Tomás Luis de Victoria (1548–1611)
- Giovanni Gabrieli (ca. 1555–1612)

The Power of Baroque Music

Baroque music reflected the growing confidence of European civilization. Elites indulged in flamboyant styles and conspicuous consumption. As a result, many Baroque composers were able to support themselves by working as court musicians for princes or high-ranking clerics. This was also an era of Scientific Revolution, lasting from 1550 to 1700, generating a new appreciation for reason and a perceived order in the world. Baroque music was elaborately textured, and it emphasized greater contrasts in tone and pace. New forms emerged such as the opera. A strong reliance on counterpoint allowed Baroque musicians to explore human emotions with an almost mathematical precision that reflected the robustly rational spirit of the age.

■ **Top to bottom:** Italian violinist and composer Antonio Vivaldi (1678–1741), circa 1725; classical violin; *Toccata No. 1 in G Major* by Alessandro Scarlatti

Baroque organ

PEOPLE OF NOTE

- Jan Pieterzoon Sweelinck (1562–1621)
- Claudio Monteverdi (1567–1643)
- Girolamo Frescobaldi (1583–1643)
- Heinrich Schütz (1585–1672)
- Francesco Cavalli (1602–1676)
- Jean-Baptiste Lully (1632–1687)
- Dieterich Buxtehude (ca.1637–1707)
- Johann Pachelbel (1653–1706)
- Arcangelo Corelli (1653–1713)
- Marin Marais (1656–1728)

- Henry Purcell (1659–1695)
- Alessandro Scarlatti (1660–1725)
- François Couperin (1668–1733)
- Tomaso Albinoni (1671–1751)
- Antonio Vivaldi (1678–1741)
- Georg Philipp Telemann (1681–1767)
- Jean-Philippe Rameau (1683–1764)
- Johann Sebastian Bach (1685–1750)
- Domenico Scarlatti (1685–1757)
- George Frideric Handel (born Georg Friedrich Händel; 1685–1759)

Bach and Handel

Johann Sebastian Bach was the most illustrious member of a remarkable family of musicians. Bach was multitalented, playing the violin, harpsichord, and organ, as well as being a good singer. He served as the musical director at several small German courts before settling down as a church musician in Leipzig in 1723. A great and prolific composer, he wrote that he made "well-ordered music in the honor of God." George Frideric Handel was a musical celebrity who worked across Europe. After years of composing in Italy and Germany, he settled in England. There he won popular acclaim for works such as his oratorio *Messiah*.

LIST OF WORKS

▮ *L'Orfeo* by Claudio Monteverdi

▮ *Armide* by Jean-Baptiste Lully

▮ *Canon in D Major* by Johann Pachelbel

▮ *Twelve Concerti Grossi, Op. 6* by Arcangelo Corelli

▮ *Dido and Aeneas* by Henry Purcell

▮ *Adagio in G Minor* by Tomaso Albinoni

▮ *The Four Seasons* by Antonio Vivaldi

▮ *Viola Concerto in G Major* by Georg Philipp Telemann

▮ *Hippolyte et Aricie* by Jean-Philippe Rameau

▮ *30 Exercises* by Domenico Scarlatti

▮ *Brandenburg Concertos* by Johann Sebastian Bach

▮ *The Art of Fugue* by Johann Sebastian Bach

▮ *St. Matthew Passion* by Johann Sebastian Bach

▮ *Water Music* by George Frideric Handel

▮ *Messiah* by George Frideric Handel

11. Concerto del Signr. Telemann,
appropriato all' Organo.

❚ Opposite page top to bottom: Statue of Johann Sebastian Bach; statue of George Frideric Händel; **This page top to bottom:** *Concerto appropriato all'Organo in G Minor* by Georg Philipp Telemann; statue of Jean-Philippe Rameau

Classical Music

The eighteenth century was the age of the Enlightenment, when the insights of the Scientific Revolution were widely diffused and human rationality was celebrated. Classical music expressed the formal elegance and simplicity of the times. Greater attention was paid to melodies, often quite catchy, and thickly textured polyphony gave way to the aural clarity of a melodic line paired with an underlying harmony. Orchestras grew in size and significance. The symphony, written expressly for orchestras, was a characteristic new musical form that appeared in this period.

▌**Top to bottom:** Gerard Dou, *Woman at the Clavichord*; the "Lépante" clavichord, Musée de la Musique, Paris

PEOPLE OF NOTE

- Giovanni Battista Sammartini (1698–1775)
- Wilhelm Friedemann Bach (1710–1784)
- Niccolo Jommelli (1714–1774)
- Christoph Willibald Gluck (1714–1787)
- Carl Philipp Emanuel Bach (1714–1788)
- Johann Stamitz (1717–1757)
- Pieter Hellendaal (1721–1799)
- François-André Danican Philidor (1726–1795)
- Antonio Soler (1729–1783)
- Franz Josef Haydn (1732–1809)
- Johann Christian Bach (1735–1782)
- Josef Myslivecek (1737–1781)
- Carl Ditters von Dittersdorf (1739–1799)
- Giovanni Paisiello (1740–1816)
- Luigi Boccherini (1743–1805)
- Carl Stamitz (1745–1801)
- Domenico Cimarosa (1749–1801)
- Antonio Salieri (1750–1825)
- Muzio Clementi (1752–1832)
- Wolfgang Amadeus Mozart (1756–1791)
- Luigi Cherubini (1760–1842)
- Ludwig van Beethoven (1770–1827)
- Johann Nepomuk Hummel (1778–1837)
- John Field (1782–1837)
- Franz Schubert (1797–1828)

■ Steel engraving of composers Mozart and Beethoven, 1882

Musical Geniuses

Franz Josef Haydn was a good-natured man who injected humor into works such as his Surprise Symphony. A prolific composer much admired in his time and since, Haydn is known as the "Father of the Symphony." Wolfgang Amadeus Mozart was a child prodigy who began composing at the age of five and publicly performing when he was six. Haydn told Mozart's father that "your son is the greatest composer known to me either in person or by reputation." In his short life Mozart produced more than six hundred compositions. Ludwig van Beethoven prefigured the arrival of Romanticism with his passionate music. Heroically, he continued to compose after becoming deaf.

LIST OF WORKS

- *Sonata No. 3* by Giovanni Battista Sammartini
- *Orpheus and Eurydice* by Christoph Willibald Gluck
- *Iphigenia in Tauris* by Christoph Willibald Gluck
- *Keyboard Sonata in D Minor* by Carl Philipp Emanuel Bach
- *Tom Jones* by François-André Danican Philidor
- *Symphony No. 45* (Farewell) by Franz Josef Haydn
- *Symphony No. 94* (Surprise) by Franz Josef Haydn
- *The Creation* by Franz Josef Haydn
- *The Barber of Seville, or The Useless Precaution* by Giovanni Paisiello
- *String Quintet in E Major* by Luigi Boccherini
- *Cello Concerto in B Flat Major* by Luigi Boccherini
- *Armida* by Antonio Salieri
- *Gradus ad Parnassum* by Muzio Clementi
- *Piano Concerto No. 24 in C Minor* by Wolfgang Amadeus Mozart
- *Symphony No. 40 in G Minor* by Wolfgang Amadeus Mozart
- *The Marriage of Figaro* by Wolfgang Amadeus Mozart
- *The Magic Flute* by Wolfgang Amadeus Mozart
- *Requiem in C Minor for Mixed Chorus* by Luigi Cherubini
- *Piano Sonata No. 8 (Sonata Pathetique)* by Ludwig van Beethoven
- *Symphony No. 3 in E Flat Major (Eroica)* by Ludwig van Beethoven
- *Symphony No. 9 in D Minor* by Ludwig van Beethoven
- *Fidelio* by Ludwig van Beethoven
- *Piano Concerto No. 2* by Johann Nepomuk Hummel
- *Winterreise* by Franz Schubert
- *Symphony No. 8 in B Minor ("the Unfinished Symphony")* by Franz Schubert

Opposite page: *Sonata per il clavicembalo o forte piano* by Antonio Salieri; **This page clockwise from bottom left:** Franz Josef Haydn; flute concert of Frederick the Great in Sanssouci by Adolph von Menzel; Franz Schubert

The Romantic Revolution

A cultural reaction against eighteenth-century rationalism, Romantic music celebrated experience and emotional expression, while experimenting with traditional forms, emphasizing melody through new and richer sounds. Romantic composers often strove for more dramatic effects and evocative moods. Some Romantic musicians became famous for their technical virtuosity, such as the violinist Niccolò Paganini. The renowned pianist Franz Liszt inspired a kind of emotional madness, dubbed "Lisztomania," in his enraptured audiences.

Opposite page top to bottom: The new opera in Paris, France, late 1800s; Franz Liszt; **This page:** A collection of classical instruments

PEOPLE OF NOTE

- Niccolò Paganini (1782–1840)
- Carl Maria von Weber (1786–1826)
- Hector Berlioz (1803–1869)
- Felix Mendelssohn (1809–1847)
- Frédéric Chopin (1810–1849)
- Robert Schumann (1810–1856)
- Franz Liszt (1811–1886)
- Jacques Offenbach (1819–1880)
- Bedrich Smetana (1824–1884)

- Anton Bruckner (1824–1896)
- Johannes Brahms (1833–1897)
- Camille Saint-Saens (1835–1921)
- Pyotr Ilyich Tchaikovsky (1840–1893)
- Antonin Dvorák (1841–1904)
- Edvard Grieg (1843–1907)
- Nikolai Rimsky-Korsakov (1844–1908)
- Gustav Mahler (1860–1911)
- Richard Strauss (1864–1949)

■ Staatsoper Opera House, Vienna

The "Total Work of Art":
Grand Opera

Dramas set to music emerged as a serious musical form around the beginning of the seventeenth century. During the Classical period, composers such as Christoph Willibald Gluck and Wolfgang Amadeus Mozart achieved fame for their operas. In the nineteenth century, the Romantic impulse inspired a vogue for lavishly produced operas featuring large casts and orchestras. Grand opera often focused on historical events that demanded spectacular sets and effects. Giacomo Meyerbeer's *Les Huguenots* (1836) and Giuseppe Verdi's *Aida* (1871) typify the dramatic splendor of grand opera. Later in the century, Ruggero Leoncavallo with *Pagliacci* (1892) and Giacomo Puccini with *Tosca* (1900) brought greater realism to opera. Richard Wagner, in the *Ring Cycle* (*Das Rheingold*, *Die Walküre*, *Siegfried*, and *Gotterdämmerung*), succeeded in uniting music, drama, and visual spectacle in a *Gesamtkunstwerk* ("total work of art").

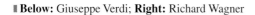
Below: Giuseppe Verdi; **Right:** Richard Wagner

PEOPLE OF NOTE

- Daniel Auber (1782–1871)
- Giacomo Meyerbeer (1791–1864)
- Gioachino Rossini (1792–1868)
- Gaetano Donizetti (1797–1848)
- Richard Wagner (1813–1883)
- Giuseppe Verdi (1813–1901)
- Charles Gounod (1818–1893)
- Jules Massenet (1842–1912)
- Ruggero Leoncavallo (1857–1919)
- Giacomo Puccini (1858–1924)

Modern Music

The advent of the twentieth century saw a reaction against the Romantic style. Composers embraced new approaches to music. Arnold Schoenberg pioneered atonality, leaving behind the traditional musical reliance on a set tone and pitch. George Antheil and others introduced the noises made by machines and other workaday sounds into their music. New technologies inspired the electroacoustic music made famously influential by composers like John Cage. Popular jazz music moved beyond American shores and inflected the work of Europeans such as Maurice Ravel and Darius Milhaud. Igor Stravinsky and Sergei Prokofiev attempted to recapture an earlier style of musical balance and discipline in their neoclassical compositions.

PEOPLE OF NOTE

- Edward Elgar (1857–1934)
- Claude Debussy (1862–1918)
- Frederick Delius (1862–1934)
- Jean Sibelius (1865–1957)
- Erik Satie (1866–1925)
- Alexander Scriabin (1872–1915)
- Ralph Vaughan Williams (1872–1958)
- Sergei Rachmaninoff (1873–1943)
- Gustav Holst (1874–1934)
- Arnold Schoenberg (1874–1951)
- Charles Ives (1874–1954)
- Maurice Ravel (1875–1937)
- Béla Bartók (1881–1945)
- Igor Stravinsky (1882–1971)
- Anton Webern (1883–1945)
- Edgard Varèse (1883–1963)
- Alban Berg (1885–1935)
- Sergei Prokofiev (1891–1953)
- Darius Milhaud (1892–1974)
- Paul Hindemith (1895–1963)
- Virgil Thomson (1896–1989)
- George Gershwin (1898–1937)
- George Antheil (1900–1959)
- Aaron Copland (1900–1990)
- Dmitri Shostakovich (1906–1975)
- John Cage (1912–1992)
- Benjamin Britten (1913–1976)
- Leonard Bernstein (1918–1990)
- Pierre Boulez (b. 1925)
- Philip Glass (b. 1937)

Opposite page: Vintage piano; **This page:** *La Bohème* by Giacomo Puccini; *Printemps* by Claude Debussy

American Music

The twentieth century was dubbed by some the "American Century." The United States flourished as an economic powerhouse and emerged from the World Wars as the dominant force in world affairs. During these years, American music came into its own. Charles Ives wrote sophisticated, sometimes experimental, music that was often influenced by American hymns and folk tunes. Virgil Thomson and Aaron Copland created a canon of recognizably American music for concertgoers. George Gershwin and Leonard Bernstein translated the vernacular of American jazz into high art. The comparative security of the United States in a violent age attracted many composers. Toward the middle of the century, American music was enriched by immigrants such as Arnold Schoenberg and Igor Stravinsky.

▌**This page:** Playbill for the Broadway musical *West Side Story* featuring music by Leonard Bernstein; **Opposite page clockwise from top left:** Composer Philip Glass, 1993; George Gershwin, 1937; Igor Stravinsky, Russian composer; Arnold Schoenberg in Los Angeles, believed to be taken in 1948; Aaron Copland School of Music at Queens College, New York

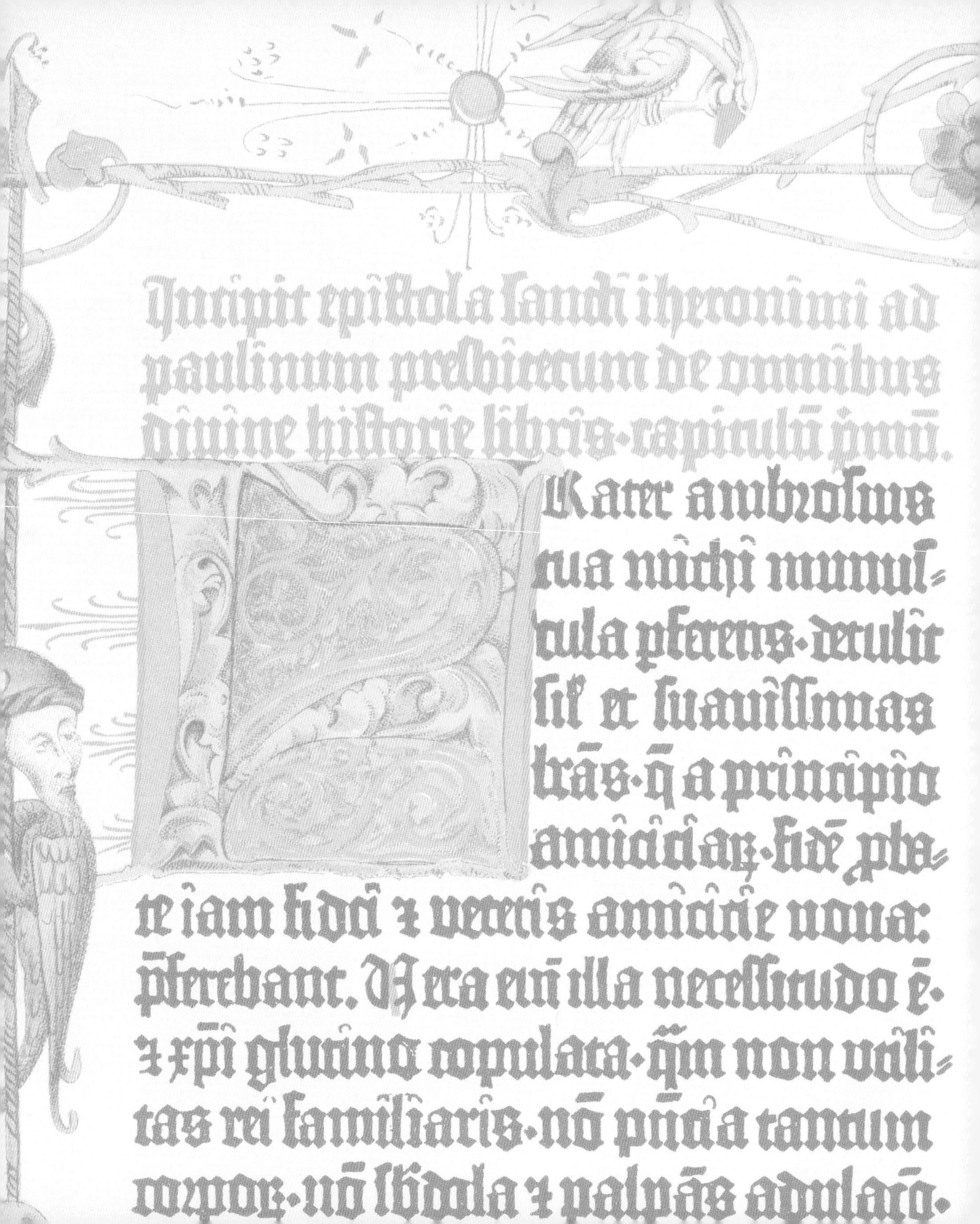

Incipit epiſtola ſancti iheronimi ad
paulinum prebiterum de omnibus
diuine hiſtorie libris·capitulũ primũ.

Rater ambroſius
tua michi munuſ
cula pferens·detulit
ſit et ſuauiſſimas
tras·ĝ a principio
amicici̅as·hđe pba
re iam fidm̅ ⁊ veteris amicicie noua:
pferebant. Vera eni̅ illa neceſſitudo e̅·
⁊ xp̅i glutino copulata·qm̅ non vtili-
tas rei familiaris·no̅ p̅nc̅ia tantum
corpor·no̅ ſbdola ⁊ palpas adulacio·

Chapter 5

Writing and the Book

Harry Scherman worked in advertising, selling mail-order goods. Scherman also loved books. In 1916, he combined business with pleasure to start the Little Leather Library with partners Maxwell Sackheim, Charles Boni, and Albert Boni. They offered leather-bound classics for $2.98 through the mail. Within a few years they sold millions of books. Then business began to taper off, and the Little Leather Library closed. In 1926, Scherman, Sackheim, and a new partner, Robert Haas, launched a new venture, the Book-of-the-Month Club. Subscribers agreed to buy four books a year, chosen from a list of works selected by the club's editorial board. As membership numbers grew into the hundreds of thousands, the gatekeeping role played by the club had an important effect on American reading habits and the book-publishing business. A Book-of-the-Month Club selection gave a book the imprimatur of respectability to millions of Americans. As Scherman explained it, the club "establishes itself as a sound selector of good books and sells by means of its own prestige. Thus, the prestige of each new title need not be built up before becoming acceptable."

By the 1950s, the Book-of-the-Month Club had established itself as the measure of middle-brow taste in American literature. Its selections by then included ten books that had won the Pulitzer Prize. The Book-of-the-Month Club may not have been the place to go for avant-garde fiction, but it had placed books in millions of homes. Few commercial ventures have been as effective in popularizing reading.

ΑΒΓΔΕΖΗΘΙΚΛΜ
ABCDEFGHIJKLMN

The Origin of Writing

Writing is an essential component of civilization, enabling records to be kept; business to be facilitated; and religion, history, and literature to be transmitted to posterity. Writing originated around 3200 B.C., when the Egyptians invented a form that the Greeks later termed hieroglyphs, or "sacred carvings." This began as a system of pictorial signs that evolved into a script. Not long after, the Sumerians of Mesopotamia developed cuneiform writing, formed by pressing the wedge-shaped ends of reeds into clay tablets.

The seafaring Phoenicians developed a twenty-two-letter alphabet based on the sounds of their language. Traders passed this on to the Greeks, who in turn transmitted it to the Romans, giving us the alphabet we use today. The Rosetta Stone, inscribed with a text from 196 B.C. written in hieroglyphics, Demotic, and Greek, made possible the deciphering of ancient Egyptian writing.

ΞΟΠΡΣΤΥΦΧΨΩ
OPQRSTUVWXYZ

Opposite page: Egyptian papyrus with illustrations and hieroglyph; **This page, clockwise from top left:** Egyptian hieroglyphs on a wall; the Rosetta Stone; ancient cuneiform writing on a clay tablet

Medieval Writing

The ancient Greeks and Romans recorded their literature on scrolls. Gradually, in the later Roman Empire, the codex, or modern book, began to emerge. The adoption of the codex by Christians for the Bible and their other writings accelerated the triumph of the book.

During the Middle Ages, books were copied by hand in monasteries. The monks who did this often "illuminated," or decorated, the pages that they worked on with elaborate and beautiful illustrations. Around A.D. 800, monks in France developed the Carolingian minuscule, which for the first time used lowercase letters, except at the beginning of sentences. This made reading much easier and made writing more attractive. The illuminations of *Les Très Riches Heures du Duc de Berry*, produced in France during the fifteenth century, often depicted everyday scenes of rural life.

▌**Opposite page, top left to bottom right:** *Les Très Riches Heures du Duc de Berry: The Nativity*; Decorative letter C as an example of monkish penmanship from the end of the ninth century; illuminated lettering in a Latin Bible of A.D. 1407 on display in Malmesbury Abbey, Wiltshire, England. It was handwritten in Belgium by Gerard Brils for reading aloud in a monastery. **This page top to bottom:** The illumination is a capital letter P because the letters following are etrus, making the word Petrus ("Peter" in Latin); ancient quill

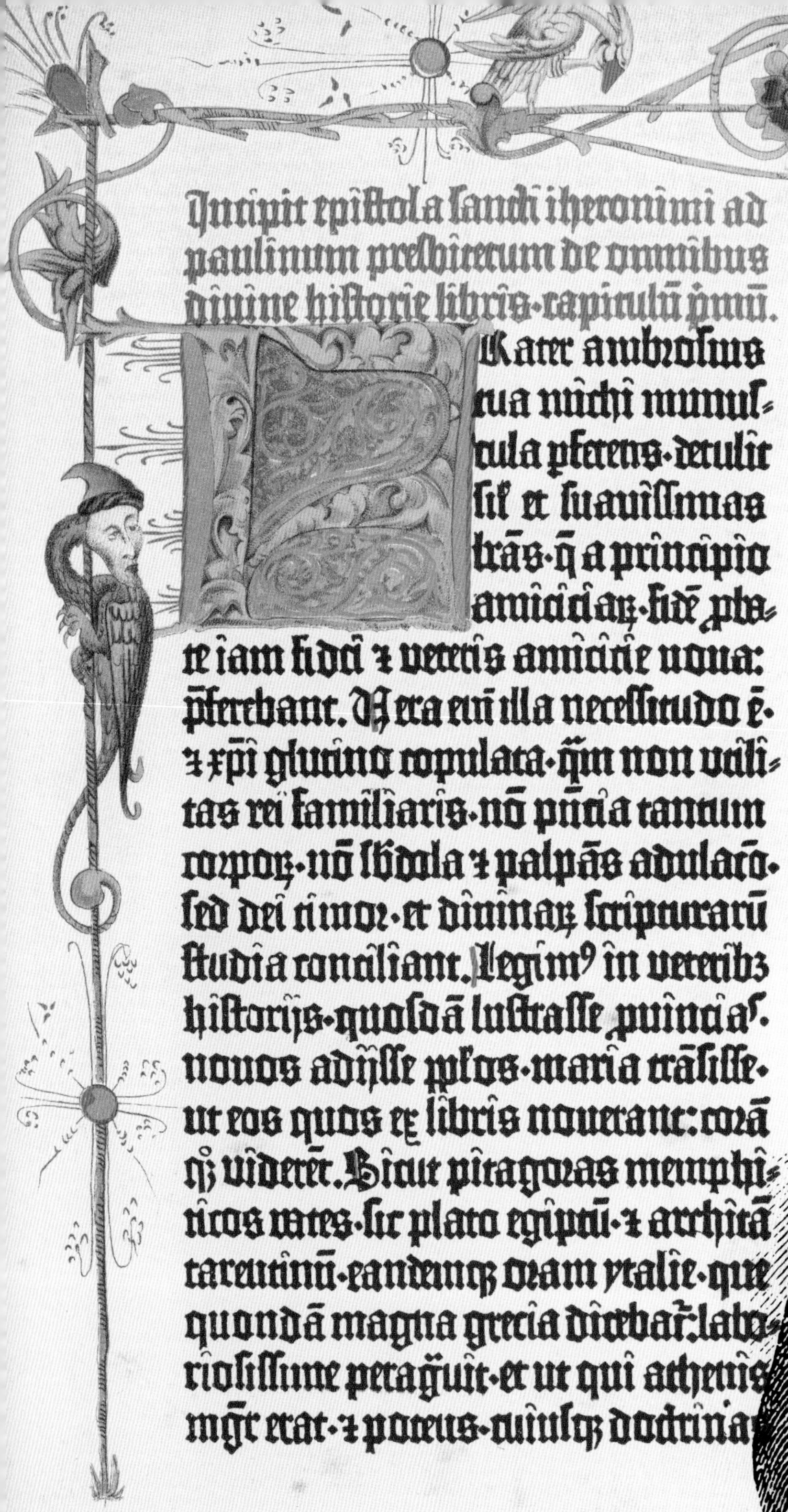

Incipit epistola sancti iheronimi ad
paulinum presbiterum de omnibus
divine historie libris·capitulū pmū.

Rater ambrosius
tua michi munus-
cula pferens·detulit
sil' et suauissimas
lras·q̃ a principio
amiciciaꝛ·side pba-
te iam fidei ⁊ veteris amicicie noua:
pferebant. Qa era enī illa necessitudo ē·
⁊ xp̄i glutino copulata·qm non vtili-
tas rei familiaris·no p̃ncia tantum
corpoꝛ·no sbdola ⁊ palpās adulaco
sed dei timor·et diuinaꝛ scripturaru
studia conciliant. legim⁹ in veteribz
historijs·quosdā lustrasse puincias·
nouos adijsse ꝓplos·maria trāsisse·
ut eos quos ex libris nouerant:corā
q̃q̃ uideret. Sicut piragoras memphi-
ticos vates·sic plato egiptu̅·⁊ archita
tarentinū·eandemqꝫ oram ytalie·que
quondā magna grecia dicebaꝩ·labo-
riosissime peraꝙit·et ut qui atheni̅s
mꝺr erat·⁊ poteus·cuiusꝗ doctrinas

INTRODUZIONE.

Rima di prender faggio alcuno dell'Opera, che hai quì prefente, ti prego, divoto Lettore, a leggere quefta brieve introduzione, che ho giudicato neceffaria a premetterfi, per difporti a ricevere quella viva, e forte impreffione, che già cagionarono quefti difcorfi nelle pieniffime udienze d'ogni claffe di perfone, maffimamente di Nobiltà, che concorrevano a udirli. E fe mai, come fpeffe volte avviene, aveffi già fcorfi quà, e là alcuni tratti, o anche qualche intero ragionamento, onde lo ftile, e le cofe ti foffer parute, o femplici, o comunali, e non aveffero adeguato la tua affpettazione, pregoti a fofpendere per brieve tempo il giudicarne, per effer quefta una forte di eloquenza nafcofta, familiare, e divota, priva di ftrepito, e d'ogni pompa, che non fa comparfa in un fubito, nè può ben fentirfi, finchè non fia entrata con qualche continuazione a penetrar dentro al cuore, a cui unicamente ella è indirizzata.

L'Opera è poftuma del P. Carl' Ambrogio Cattaneo della Compagnia di Gesù, morto in Milano fua Patria nel mille fettecento cinque in concetto univerfale di fegnalate virtù, maffimamente di zelo Appoftolico nel tirar l'anime a Dio, e in mantenerle perfeveranti, e fempre più avanzate nella via della falute. Incredibili però furono gli ftudj, e le invenzioni, e gli ftenti, con cui quefto fervente operario adoperoffi con ogni condizion di perfone in sì arduo, e falutevole miniftero. Bafti il dire, che, effendo egli di robuftiffimo temperamento, le grandi, ed ecceffive fatiche, fingolarmente nel

a 2   dare

▌**Opposite page:** Page of the 42-line Gutenberg Bible printed in 1455; antique nineteenth-century engraving of a portrait of Johannes Gutenberg, German goldsmith and printer; **This page:** First page of an Italian book, 1700

Printed Books

The Chinese invented printing early in the Middle Ages, and by the middle of the fourteenth century, thanks to the gradual spread of this technology, Europeans were making prints using wood blocks. Around 1450, Johannes Gutenberg of Mainz, Germany, invented a system of printing from movable type made from metal. The use of this durable, reusable type revolutionized printing. In 1455, Gutenberg released his Bible, at once beautifully printed and much less expensive than hand-copied books.

The new printing exploded across Europe. By 1500, more than one thousand printers were working in Europe, and since Gutenberg's day they had published more than 9 million books. Much of this avalanche of printed words was religious in nature and helped lay the foundations of the Reformation and Counter-Reformation. The large reading public stimulated by the easy access to books helped foster the intellectual revolution of the Renaissance.

Chapter 6

History

Edward Gibbon took some time to discover his life's work. His father owned an estate, but the younger Gibbon never showed any inclination to settle down as a country gentleman. Early in life he was shaken by religious enthusiasms, and the experience left him famously cool to the conventionalities of the Christian faith. He had always been an apt student and enjoyed reading. An early essay on the study of literature marked him as a potential man of letters. The decisive moment in Gibbon's life came during a visit to Rome in 1764. He was overwhelmed by the remains of the mighty Roman Empire. As he wrote many years later: "I can neither forget nor express the strong emotions which agitated my mind as I first approached and entered the eternal city. After a sleepless night, I trod with a lofty step the ruins of the Forum; each memorable spot where Romulus stood, or Tully [Cicero] spoke, or Caesar fell, was at once present to my eye; and several days of intoxication were lost or enjoyed before I could descend to a cool and minute investigation." One night Gibbon received his inspiration: "It was at Rome, on the fifteenth of October, 1764, as I sat musing amidst the ruins of the Capitol, while the barefooted fryars were singing Vespers in the temple of Jupiter, that the idea of writing the decline and fall of the City first started to my mind." Gibbon would go on to demonstrate that the best history is literature of the highest order.

The Ancient World

The origins of the modern Western world lie in the ancient Near East. The Sumerian city-states emerged by 3000 B.C. along the Tigris and Euphrates rivers in Mesopotamia. Simultaneously, Egyptian civilization developed along the Nile River and endured for three millennia. The Mesopotamians and Egyptians created an international system that eventually included peoples who lived to the west.

The ancient Greeks inhabited fractious city-states. The spirit of individualism and inquiry nurtured in these conditions inspired the foundations of Western political liberty, philosophy, and art. As Greek power declined, Alexander the Great of Macedon conquered the city-states and spread Greek culture throughout the Near Eastern heartland of civilization as far as India. The Romans, in turn, defeated the heirs of Alexander, creating an empire that transmitted Greek ideals to the West, from Rome to the borders of Scotland.

The Great Sphinx and the pyramids of Giza are among the most recognizable symbols of the civilization of ancient Egypt.

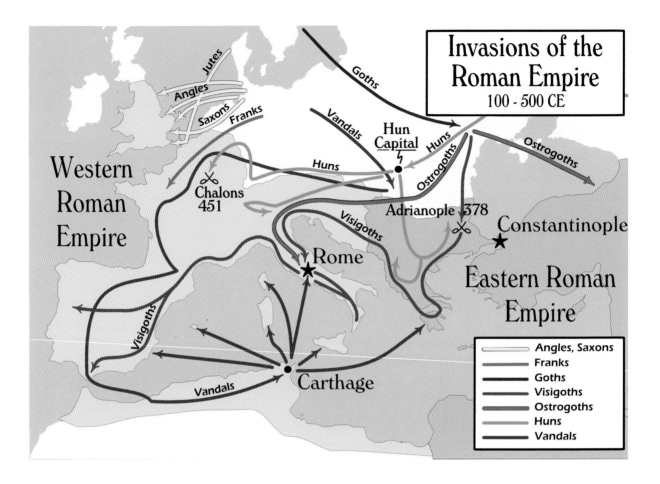

The Medieval World: Invasions

For most of human history, civilization was a precarious achievement. Waves of less-developed people from outside the limits of settled society were continually tempted to raid in search of booty, or to invade in search of land. The mighty Roman Empire eventually fell before migrating bands of Germanic barbarians hoping to share in the goods of civilization, unaware that they were destroying the fragile social fabric that sustained that bounty.

After centuries of turmoil, Charlemagne rebuilt an empire in Western Europe that promised to restore stability and prosperity. But civil strife and devastating raids by Scandinavian Vikings brought renewed chaos. Norman descendants of Viking settlers in France conquered England in 1066. A devastating Mongol invasion threatened Europe in the thirteenth century. Only internal dissensions diverted the fearsome horsemen of the steppes.

Opposite page: Map of the "barbarian" invasions of the Roman Empire showing the major incursions from A.D. 100 to 500; **This page clockwise from top left:** Tamerlane, or Tamburlaine (1336–1405), Tartar conqueror, c. 1370; vintage engraving with detail of the Bayeux Tapestry, showing the Coronation of King Harold; vintage engraving from 1883 of two Viking longships engaged in battle; vintage engraving depicting the battle between Japanese warriors and a Mongol invasion force in the thirteenth century

❚ An engraving showing King John of England signing the Magna Carta in 1215

The Medieval World: Revival

After the year 1000, Western Europe began to recover from the collapse of the Carolingian Empire. Feudalism and manorialism provided a new political and economic foundation for society. Towns and trade began to revive. The twelfth and thirteenth centuries saw a stunning burst of creativity that included the founding of the medieval universities and the building of the great Gothic cathedrals. This was the age of the Crusades, which reintroduced Europe to the East, and the Magna Carta, which laid the foundations of liberty in England.

In the fourteenth and fifteenth centuries, medieval civilization was ravaged by the Black Death (bubonic plague), which killed nearly half the people of Europe, and wasting conflicts like the Hundred Years War between England and France. Renewal came with the Renaissance, which rediscovered classical civilization, and the Reformation, which challenged religious tradition.

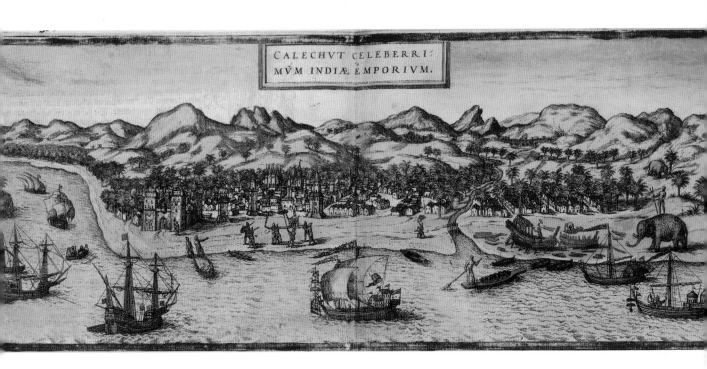

CALECHVT CELEBERRI: MVM INDIÆ EMPORIVM.

▌**Above:** A panorama of Calicut, on the Malabar Coast, shows several types of ships, shipbuilding, net fishing, dinghy traffic, and a rugged, sparsely populated interior during the spice trade; **Below left:** Vintage engraving showing King Henry V of England at the Battle of Agincourt in 1415 during the Hundred Years War; **Below right:** An engraving from the 1580s of Martin Luther, leader of the great religious revolt of the sixteenth century in Germany

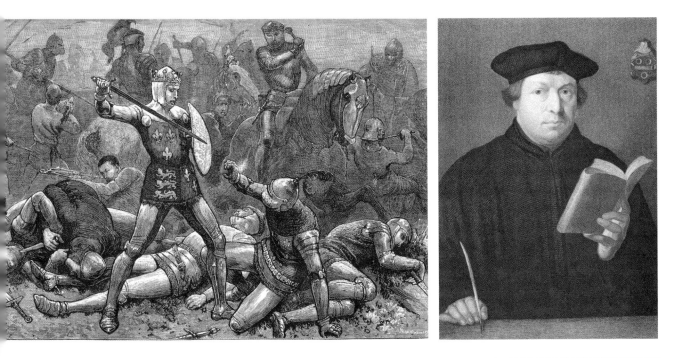

The Modern World: Britain

The foundation of the British Empire was sea power. British naval power, rooted in its struggles against Spain and the invading Armada in the sixteenth century, grew stronger in the seventeenth century and nurtured a flourishing commerce. By the eighteenth century, the British navy was the strongest in the world, and it protected an empire that had spread around the world, from India to America.

The wealth generated by Britain's commercial success contributed to British leadership in the Industrial Revolution. By the mid-nineteenth century, inventions such as Richard Arkwright's spinning machine, James Watt's steam engine, and George Stephenson's locomotive helped make Britain the "workshop of the world." The new industrial techniques soon spread throughout Europe and to America, transforming the economy of the Western world.

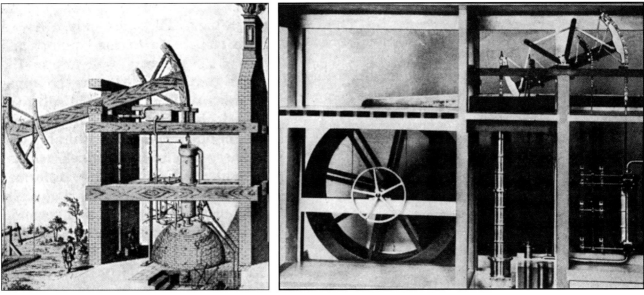

■ Thomas Newcomen created the first practical steam engine for pumping water. The Newcomen steam engine was probably developed around 1710.

■ Improving on the design of the 1712 Newcomen engine, the Watt steam engine, developed from 1763 to 1775, was the next great step in the development of the steam engine.

■ The introduction of the spinning mule into cotton production processes helped drastically increase industrial consumption of cotton. This example is the only one in existence made by inventor Samuel Crompton.

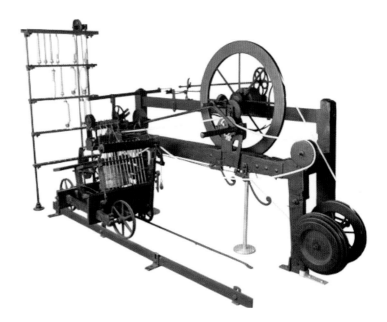

An Age of Revolution

The American Revolution began as a protest against British "taxation without representation" and concluded as the first defense of natural rights, "life, liberty, and the pursuit of happiness." War broke out in 1775 and independence was declared in 1776, but it would take long years of bloody fighting and the intervention of France and other great powers before the United States achieved international recognition with the Treaty of Paris in 1783.

A fiscal crisis led to the French Revolution in 1789. At first France settled into a constitutional monarchy, but internal dissensions, war, and the rise of the radical Jacobins led to the Reign of Terror in 1793–1794, when King Louis XVI and thousands of others were guillotined. Eventually the dictator Napoleon Bonaparte seized power in France, though a coalition of European powers ended his reign in 1815. Inspired by the American and French revolutions, Simón Bolívar led Latin Americans to independence from Spain.

■ **Opposite page:** Guillotine; steel engraving from
1870 of Simón Bolívar (1783–1830); **This page top
to bottom:** Vintage watercolor engraving by Paul
Revere of the Boston Massacre, March 5, 1770;
Napoleon Bonaparte in the coup d'état of 18 Bru-
maire in Saint-Cloud

Nineteenth-Century War

The conclusion of the Napoleonic Wars in 1815 ushered in a century of unprecedented European peace. Although no general wars disturbed the continent, regional conflicts erupted from time to time. In the Crimean War of 1854–1856, the British and French helped the Turks stave off an attack by Russia. The Franco-Prussian War of 1870–1871 enabled Otto von Bismarck to engineer the unification of Germany.

The Europeans fought many colonial wars. The Sepoy Rebellion by native troops against the East India Company in 1857–1858 was bloodily suppressed and led to direct British rule in India. The American Civil War of 1861–1865 cost 600,000 lives but ended Southern secession and abolished slavery in the United States. It was also the first war in which railroads played a key role in transporting troops.

▌**This page top to bottom:** Ulysses S. Grant Memorial with Old Glory flying in the background; steam engine like the ones used to transport troops during the American Civil War

▌**Opposite page top to bottom:** Disarming the 11th irregular cavalry at Berhampore during the Indian mutiny of 1857; the final assault of the French brought about the capture of Sevastopol during the Crimean War after one of the most memorable sieges of the nineteenth century

▌**This page left to right:** Atomic bombing of Nagasaki, Japan, on August 9, 1945; trenches on the Western Front; German Albatros D.III biplane fighters of Jasta 11 at Douai, France; British Mark IV tank crossing a trench; Vickers machine-gun crew with gas masks; British battleship HMS *Irresistible* sinking after striking a mine

▌**Opposite page top to bottom:** Lancaster bombers from the Battle of Britain in World War II; statue of Mahatma Gandhi in the city of Udaipur, India

World War and Revolution

The outbreak of World War I in 1914 inaugurated a period of unprecedented violence and upheaval. By the time the war ended in 1918, 10 million people were dead; the German, Austro-Hungarian, Ottoman Turkish, and Russian empires had collapsed; and the United States had emerged as a world power. The Russian Revolution of 1917 gave birth to the first totalitarian state, the Communist Soviet Union.

World War II was even more destructive. Some 70 million people perished in Asia and Europe. Nazi Germany attempted genocide against the Jews in the Holocaust. The war in Asia ended when the United States dropped atomic bombs on Japan. In the aftermath of the war, India gained its independence from a weakened British Empire. Mao Zedong led his Communist forces to victory over their Nationalist opponents in 1949.

The Cold War

The end of World War II did not bring peace. A Cold War developed between the United States and its Western European allies, and the Soviet Union, which now controlled most of Eastern Europe. The United States attempted to contain Communist expansion through policies like the Marshall Plan and institutions like NATO (North Atlantic Treaty Organization). Both sides sought influence in the new nations of the Third World.

During the Korean War (1950–1953), the United States and the United Nations successfully defended the independence of South Korea. During the Vietnam War (1965–1973), the United States failed to create a viable South Vietnamese state as a bulwark against Asian communism and nationalism. The Arab-Israeli wars reflected Cold War tensions, but by 1989 the Cold War was drawing to a close. In Germany, protestors tore down the Berlin Wall. In China, however, the government gunned down pro-democracy students in Tiananmen Square on June 4, 1989, effectively ending the movement toward democracy.

▌**This page top to bottom:** A gun crew checks their equipment near the Kum River, Korea, July 15, 1950; Major Crandall's UH-1D helicopter climbs skyward after discharging a load of infantrymen on a search-and-destroy mission; **Opposite page clockwise from top left:** People atop the Berlin Wall near the Brandenburg Gate on November 9, 1989; the Gate of Heavenly Peace on Tiananmen Square; President Harry S. Truman signs a proclamation declaring a national emergency that initiates U.S. involvement in the Korean War; Israeli prime minister Yitzhak Rabin, U.S. president Bill Clinton, and PLO chairman Yasser Arafat

Chapter 7

Literature

Mary Shelley was the daughter of the philosopher William Godwin and the feminist Mary Wollstonecraft, who died ten days after she was born. Mary Wollstonecraft Godwin received a good, if unconventional, education from her father. In 1814, the Romantic poet Percy Bysshe Shelley visited William Godwin. Though Percy Shelley was married and his wife was pregnant, he and the sixteen-year-old Mary began a passionate love affair. The two eloped to France, bringing along Mary's half-sister Claire Clairmont. Mary became pregnant, but the baby died within a month of its birth. However, Mary was soon pregnant again, giving birth to a son in January 1816.

A few months later, Shelley's unconventional family traveled to Lake Geneva to spend the summer with the poet Lord Byron, who had impregnated Claire Clairmont. One rainy evening, the Shelleys, Byron, and Byron's physician John Polidori amused themselves by reading aloud from a book of German ghost stories and discussing the attempt of the naturalist Erasmus Darwin to reanimate dead tissue through electricity. Byron suggested that they all write a horror story. This inspired a frightful dream in Mary, combining the effects of the stories she had heard and her grief for her lost child. "I saw the pale student of unhallowed arts kneeling beside the thing he had put together. I saw the hideous phantasm of a man stretched out, and then . . . show signs of life." Encouraged by Percy Shelley, Mary soon turned her dream into a novel. Like the novel itself, the story of the origin of Frankenstein is a commentary on the mystery of creation.

▌*Aeneas Flees Burning Troy* by Federico Barocci

Classical Literature

The literary mainsprings of Western civilization were the Greek poet Homer's *Iliad* and *Odyssey*. *The Iliad*, set during the Trojan War, details the tragic events following a quarrel between the Greek hero Achilles and King Agamemnon. *The Odyssey* describes Odysseus's attempt to return home to his wife and son after the war. Brilliant in their descriptive power and force of characterization, these poems shaped Greek literature for centuries. Alexander the Great liked to think of himself as a reborn Achilles and kept a copy of *The Iliad* by his bed. The Roman poet Virgil (70–19 B.C.) ambitiously decided to create his own epic poem about the origins of the Roman people. *The Aeneid* follows the flight of Aeneas and a small band of Trojan refugees from the wreck of their city to a new home in Italy.

▌**Left to right:** An engraving showing an ancient bard telling stories; statue of Cicero

Nos autem beatam vitam in

animi securitate et in omnium

vacatione munerum ponimus.

De Natura Deorum (I, 53)

From Latin to the Vernacular

From the end of the Roman Empire, Latin was the language of church and literature. In the fourteenth century, however, three great works were written in the vernacular, aiming to reach larger audiences and setting the stage for the national literatures that would follow. *The Divine Comedy* of Dante Alighieri (1265–1321) takes the author on a journey through Hell, Purgatory, and Heaven. The poet Virgil guides Dante through Hell and Purgatory, while his lost love Beatrice takes him through Heaven. *The Divine Comedy* is both an allegory on the soul's progression to salvation and a scintillating compendium of medieval learning. Vastly different in spirit is Giovanni Boccaccio's (1313–1375) *Decameron*. Fleeing the Black Death of 1348, ten young people tell each other a hundred tales of love that often display a graphic lack of sentimentality. *The Canterbury Tales* by Geoffrey Chaucer (ca. 1343–1400) tells the stories of a disparate group of pilgrims, depicting a rich cross-section of medieval life.

▌Dante

▌Italian calligraphy of a section of Dante's *Inferno*

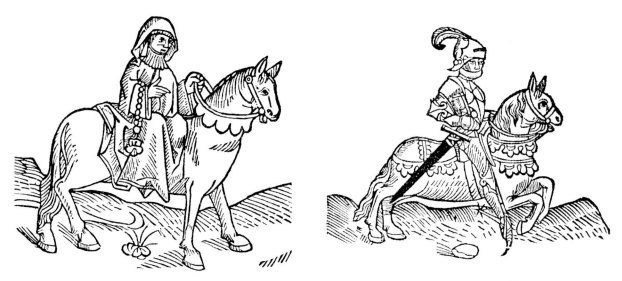

■ The Prioress and the Knight from Chaucer's *The Canterbury Tales* (woodcut from the 1485 edition)

■ Equestrian statue of Can Grande della Scala from the seventh tale of the *Decameron*

Chivalric Romances

Medieval knights loved to hear poems celebrating their warlike profession. None satisfied as much as *The Song of Roland*, which appeared around the year 1100. Set in the days of Emperor Charlemagne, *The Song of Roland* tells of a military encounter in which Count Roland is treacherously beset by hordes of Saracen warriors. Too proud to sound his horn for help, Roland and his men heroically fight to the last man, along the way dispatching vast numbers of enemies in satisfyingly gruesome ways. The rise of courtly love in the twelfth century added a note of romance to chivalric literature. In such tales, heroic knights engage in spectacular feats to win the hearts of their lady-loves. During the Middle Ages, tales about King Arthur were immensely popular, effectively combining doomed lovers with knightly derring-do. Sir Thomas Malory (ca. 1405–1471) compiled the best-known collection of stories about King Arthur, Queen Guinevere, Sir Lancelot, and the Knights of the Round Table: *Le Morte d'Arthur*.

LIST OF WORKS

▪ *The Song of Roland*

▪ *Parzival* by Wolfram von Eschenbach

▪ *Tristan en Prose*

▪ *Sir Gawain and the Green Knight*

▪ *Le Morte d'Arthur* by Thomas Malory

▪ **Top to bottom:** Arthur pulling the sword from the stone; ruins of Tintagel Castle in Cornwall believed to be the home of King Arthur

y endroit dit le conte que quant
les lespres du tornoiemet furt
fuces le rop artus senretorna
vert somerep lie et ioreur de ce
que lon comenrcent auoit eu

■ Medieval illuminated document of Lancelot and Tristan in the Tournament at Louvezep

Above: Page from Shakespeare; **Opposite page left to right:** Ben Jonson; playbill for a performance of Christopher Marlowe's *Doctor Faustus*

Early Modern English Drama

In the late sixteenth and early seventeenth centuries, English drama flourished, producing many masterpieces of world literature. The theater at this time was a democratic form of art; audiences ranged from the aristocracy to the ordinary person on the street. In venues such as London's Globe Theatre, a well-to-do patron could purchase a seat or a place in a box, or jostle with the hoi polloi in the pit. Theatrical companies had an insatiable demand for new plays because these were presented as parts of extensive repertories, rather than being performed consecutively for days or weeks at a time. Playwrights rose to this challenge for material. Christopher Marlowe (1564–1593) began a brilliant career before being killed in a fight. Ben Jonson (1572–1637) gained fame as a writer of comedies. The greatest of these dramatists was William Shakespeare (1564–1616), who excelled at both comedy and tragedy, providing succeeding generations with "such stuff as dreams are made on."

LIST OF WORKS

- ▌ *Tamburlaine the Great* by Christopher Marlowe
- ▌ *Volpone* by Ben Jonson
- ▌ *A Midsummer Night's Dream* by William Shakespeare
- ▌ *Hamlet* by William Shakespeare
- ▌ *Macbeth* by William Shakespeare

Talking and eloquence are not the same thing: to speak, and to speak well, are two things. A fool may talk, but a wise man speaks.

Ben Jonson
Timber: Or, Discoveries

Continental Literature in the Sixteenth and Eighteenth Centuries

❚ Erasmus of Rotterdam

While Shakespeare was staging his great plays, Miguel de Cervantes (1547–1616) was creating the modern novel. A former soldier who had been disabled at the Battle of Lepanto, Cervantes satirized popular chivalric romances through his lovable character Don Quixote, who, with his squire and sidekick Sancho Panza, attempts to find knightly romance and adventure in a distinctly unheroic Spain. During the reign of Louis XIV, the comic writer Jean-Baptiste Poquelin (1622–1673), better known as Molière, and the tragedian Jean Racine (1639–1699) helped spark a golden age in French drama. In the eighteenth century, the Enlightenment sage Voltaire caused a sensation with his picaresque novel *Candide*. Voltaire uses this form to mount a scorching denunciation of the political and religious authorities of the day. Even as the hero Candide lurches from one disaster to another, his teacher Pangloss declares, "All is for the best in the best of all possible worlds." Jean-Jacques Rousseau in his *Julie* celebrated feeling over reason and prepared the way for Romanticism.

LIST OF WORKS

❚ *The Ingenious Gentleman Don Quixote de la Mancha* by Miguel de Cervantes

❚ *The Misanthrope* by Molière

❚ *Andromaque* by Jean Racine

❚ *Candide* by Voltaire

❚ *Julie, or the New Heloise* by Jean-Jacques Rousseau

❚ Engraving from *The Praise of Folly*

Top to bottom, left to right: Sculpture of Don Quixote and Sancho Panza; adventure with the windmills from *Don Quixote* (engraving); illustration of two monkeys chasing their lovers from Voltaire's *Candide*

Eighteenth-Century English Literature

Literature flourished in eighteenth-century England, nurtured by a rich literary tradition and the wealth generated by Britain's burgeoning empire. Alexander Pope (1688–1744) was the greatest of England's Neoclassical poets, effortlessly dashing off such quotable lines as "For fools rush in where angels fear to tread." Samuel Johnson (1709–1784) was a multifaceted man of letters, but his most famous work was *A Dictionary of the English Language*, the first truly comprehensive English lexicography. Daniel Defoe (ca. 1659–1731) was a journalist who turned his reportorial skills to fictional use in his novels about castaways and the 1665 Great Plague of London. Though Jonathan Swift (1667–1745) more than held his own as an essayist in an age of great essayists, his most enduring legacy is his fanciful tale of Lemuel Gulliver's voyages. In the comic hands of Henry Fielding (1707–1754) and Laurence Sterne (1713–1768), the English novel achieved a richly boisterous maturity.

LIST OF WORKS

▮ *The Rape of the Lock* by Alexander Pope

▮ *Robinson Crusoe* by Daniel Defoe

▮ *Gulliver's Travels* by Jonathan Swift

▮ *The History of Tom Jones, a Foundling* by Henry Fielding

▮ *The Life and Opinions of Tristram Shandy, Gentleman* by Laurence Sterne

The Roast Beef of Old England
Lyrics by Henry Fielding

When mighty Roast Beef was the Englishman's food,

It ennobled our brains and enriched our blood.

Our soldiers were brave and our courtiers were good

Oh! the Roast Beef of old England,

And old English Roast Beef!

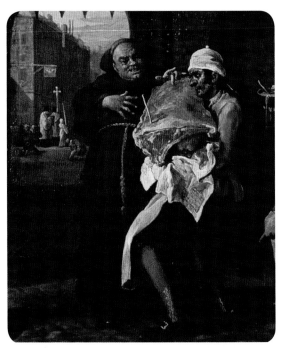

▮ **This page:** *The Roast Beef of Old England* by William Hogarth; **Opposite page:** Guy Noel Pocock's illustration of *Robinson Crusoe* from a 1910 edition of the book by Daniel Defoe © The Art Archive at Art Resource, NY

Jane Austen and the Brontë Sisters

Men did not have literature to themselves in the eighteenth and nineteenth centuries. In the eighteenth century Fanny Burney (1752–1840) wrote social comedies about the English aristocracy, while Ann Radcliffe (1764–1823) helped pioneer the Gothic thriller. Jane Austen (1775–1817) drew on the inspiration of these predecessors while carving out her own unique niche as the master commentator on manners and marriage among the English gentry. Aware of but rejecting literary Romanticism, Austen wrote with penetrating humor and clear-eyed intelligence about the challenges facing bright young women negotiating the social shoals and rapids barring the way to connubial bliss. The Brontë sisters, born around the time Austen passed from the scene, embraced a Romantic vision of relations between men and women. Sisters Charlotte (1816–1855), Emily (1818–1848), and Anne Brontë (1820–1849), during their tragically brief lives, all wrote books about brave women and their brooding men that captured the imaginations of readers then and now.

▮ Portrait of Jane Austen by her sister
Cassandra

LIST OF WORKS

▮ *Pride and Prejudice* by Jane Austen

▮ *Persuasion* by Jane Austen

▮ *Jane Eyre* by Charlotte Brontë

▮ *Wuthering Heights* by Emily Brontë

▮ *The Tenant of Wildfell Hall* by Anne Brontë

▌Portrait of the Brontë Sisters,
by Patrick Branwell Brontë. Left to
right, Anne, Emily, and Charlotte.

Nineteenth-Century Women Authors

Women authors were immensely popular in the nineteenth century, much to the consternation of male writers like Nathaniel Hawthorne, who complained about the "damned mob of scribbling women" whose works drove his out of the bookstore windows. Most of these women wrote popular romantic fiction, but many blazed new literary trails. Mary Shelley (1797–1851) combined horror and science fiction in her famous tale of Victor Frankenstein and the monster he created. Elizabeth Gaskell (1810–1865) wrote a socially conscious study of industrial conditions in *Mary Barton*. Harriet Beecher Stowe (1811–1896) helped precipitate the Civil War with her novel about the travails of Uncle Tom. Mary Anne Evans (1819–1880), who used the pen name George Eliot, defied Victorian conventions in her private life, while establishing herself as a popular and respected author. Very different in temperament was the American poet Emily Dickinson (1830–1886), who lived a secluded life in her family home, leaving most of her poems to be published by friends after her death.

LIST OF WORKS

▮ *Frankenstein, or The Modern Prometheus* by Mary Shelley

▮ *Mary Barton* by Elizabeth Gaskell

▮ *Middlemarch: A Study of Provincial Life* by George Eliot

▮ *Uncle Tom's Cabin; or Life Among the Lowly*
  by Harriet Beecher Stowe

▮ *The Poems of Emily Dickinson* by Emily Dickinson

I saw—with shut eyes, but acute mental vision—I saw the pale student of unhallowed arts kneeling beside the thing he had put together. I saw the hideous phantasm of a man stretched out, and then, on the working of some powerful engine, show signs of life and stir with an uneasy, half-vital motion. Frightful must it be, for supremely frightful would be the effect of any human endeavor to mock the stupendous mechanism of the Creator of the world.

Mary Shelley

▌ **This page:** Portrait of Mary Shelley; part of the original manuscript of *Frankenstein*

▌ **Opposite page:** Photograph of Emily Dickinson; Tom and Maggie Tulliver from *The Mill on the Floss* by George Eliot

Leopards, tygers play,
Round her as she lay;
While the lion old,
Bow'd his mane of gold.

And her bosom lick,
And upon her neck,
From his eyes of flame,
Ruby tears there came;

While the lioness
Loos'd her slender dress,
And naked they convey'd
To caves the sleeping maid.

The Little Girl Found

All the night in woe,
Lyca's parents go:
Over vallies deep,
While the desarts weep.

Tired and woe-begone,
Hoarse with making moan:
Arm in arm seven days
They trac'd the desert ways.

Seven nights they sleep,
Among shadows deep:
And dream they see their child
Starv'd in desart wild.

Pale thro' pathless ways
The fancied image strays.

Famish'd

▌Page from *Songs of Innocence* by William Blake. Lessing J. Rosenwald Collection, Library of Congress. Copyright © 2012 the William Blake Archive. Used with permission.

British Romantic Poets

The Romantics rejected eighteenth-century rationalism and instead exalted individual self-expression. William Wordsworth (1770–1850) wrote that poetry was "the spontaneous overflow of powerful feelings." He and his friend Samuel Taylor Coleridge (1772–1834) launched the Romantic Movement in British poetry with their 1798 collaboration *Lyrical Ballads*. Following the beat of his own drummer, the deeply religious poet and printer William Blake (1757–1827) illustrated and published volumes of his own poems, writing, "I must create a system or be enslaved by another man's." Percy Bysshe Shelley (1792–1822) and George Gordon Byron, Sixth Baron Byron (1788–1824), embodied the Romantic ideals that they celebrated in their poetry, simultaneously scandalizing and fascinating contemporaries with their openly unconventional lives. Both sealed their legends by dying young: Shelley drowned in a boating accident, and Lord Byron perished of disease (and mistreatment by his doctors) while serving as a volunteer in the Greek War of Independence. John Keats (1795–1821) lived more quietly but was also carried away prematurely by tuberculosis.

Ode to a Nightingale

by John Keats

Thou wast not born for death, immortal Bird!
No hungry generations tread thee down;
The voice I hear this passing night was heard
In ancient days by emperor and clown:

The Rime of the Ancient Mariner
Samuel Taylor Coleridge, 1798

And a good south wind sprung up behind;
The Albatross did follow,
And every day, for food or play,
Came to the mariners' hollo!

In mist or cloud, on mast or shroud,
It perched for vespers nine;
Whiles all the night, through fog-smoke white,
Glimmered the white Moon-shine.'

▌ Illustration of Samuel Taylor Coleridge's "Rime of the Ancient Mariner" by Gustave Doré

LIST OF WORKS

▌ *Songs of Innocence and of Experience* by William Blake

▌ *Lyrical Ballads, with a Few Other Poems* by William Wordsworth and Samuel Taylor Coleridge

▌ *Childe Harold's Pilgrimage* by Lord Byron

▌ *Prometheus Unbound* by Percy Bysshe Shelley

▌ *Lamia, Isabella, The Eve of St. Agnes and Other Poems* by John Keats

▌ **This page left to right:** Page proofs of Balzac's novel *Béatrix*; *Victor Hugo Haunted by the Goddess of War* (engraving); **Opposite page top to bottom:** Scene from Dickens's *A Christmas Carol*; scenes from *Oliver Twist*

Nineteenth-Century Novelists

The nineteenth century was a golden age for the novel. A large literate public demonstrated an almost insatiable appetite for popular works of fiction. In England, many novels were serialized and published in installments, keeping readers enthralled for months or even years. William Makepeace Thackeray (1811–1863) satirized British society in the aptly named *Vanity Fair*. Charles Dickens (1812–1870) was the master of the serialized novel. From the 1830s through the 1860s he was a cultural institution in Great Britain. He created vividly memorable characters, some of whom, such as Ebenezer Scrooge, have entered the English dictionary. In France, Honoré de Balzac (1799–1850) created an enormous cycle of more than ninety stories and novels dissecting French society that he called *The Human Comedy*. Gustave Flaubert (1821–1880) created a scandal with his precisely observed and worded study of a fallen woman. Victor Hugo (1802–1885) combined a passion for social justice with a Romantic sensibility in his greatest works.

LIST OF WORKS

▌ *Eugénie Grandet* by Honoré de Balzac

▌ *Vanity Fair: A Novel Without a Hero* by William Makepeace Thackeray

▌ *Madame Bovary* by Gustave Flaubert

▌ *Great Expectations* by Charles Dickens

▌ *Les Misérables* by Victor Hugo

A pure hand needs

Nineteenth-Century American Literature

American literature came into its own in the nineteenth century. The first American author to attain an international reputation was Washington Irving (1783–1859), who created such memorable characters as Ichabod Crane and Rip Van Winkle. James Fenimore Cooper (1789–1851) innovated with popular novels set on the frontier. His intrepid scout Leatherstocking became the archetype for the American Western hero. The middle of the century saw an American literary renaissance that produced a number of masterpieces. Nathaniel Hawthorne (1804–1864) explored the nature of good and evil in works often set against the background of his native New England. Herman Melville (1819–1891) received acclaim for tales of nautical adventure, but baffled readers with *Moby-Dick*. Walt Whitman (1819–1892) poetically celebrated both himself and his expanding nation in *Leaves of Grass*. Samuel Langhorne Clemens (1835–1910) emerged from the American West and as Mark Twain made its vernacular literarily respectable. Known as a humorist, Twain did not fear to tackle controversial topics like racism, declaring, "Against the assault of laughter nothing can stand."

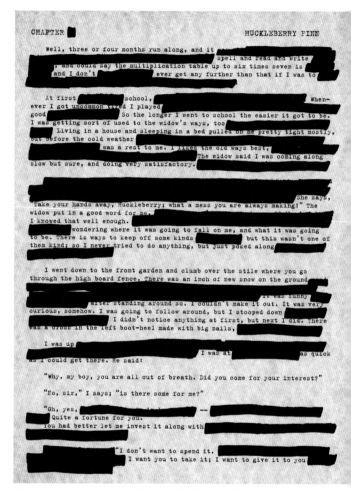

▮ Censored page of Mark Twain's *Huckleberry Finn*

no glove to cover it

Nathaniel Hawthorne, *The Scarlet Letter*

LIST OF WORKS

▮ *The Last of the Mohicans: A Narrative of 1757* by James Fenimore Cooper

▮ *The Scarlet Letter* by Nathaniel Hawthorne

▮ *Moby-Dick: or, The Whale* by Herman Melville

▮ *Leaves of Grass* by Walt Whitman

▮ *Adventures of Huckleberry Finn* by Mark Twain

There is a wisdom that is woe;

but there is a woe

that is madness.

Herman Melville, *Moby-Dick*

Nineteenth-Century Drama

Drama in the early nineteenth century was heavily influenced by Romanticism and often suffused with melodrama. Victor Hugo's 1830 play *Hernani* exemplifies this with a plot full of political and sexual intrigue, ending with a spate of suicides. Later in the century, dramatists turned to a more realistic presentation of the human condition. The Norwegian playwright Henrik Ibsen (1828–1906) led the way with dramas that explore the struggles of individuals to escape the stifling constraints of society. Ibsen's Swedish contemporary, August Strindberg (1849–1912), brought a Darwinian perspective to his realism, attempting to portray people as products of their familial and social environment. Anton Chekov (1860–1904) was a master of subtle character studies in late-Tsarist Russia. In England, Oscar Wilde (1854–1900) and George Bernard Shaw (1856–1950) used laughter to satirize Victorian society. With lapidary wit, Wilde skewered the mores of the upper classes, while Shaw confronted audiences with such problematic topics as prostitution.

LIST OF WORKS

▮ *A Doll's House* by Henrik Ibsen

▮ *Miss Julie* by August Strindberg

▮ *Mrs. Warren's Profession* by George Bernard Shaw

▮ *The Importance of Being Earnest* by Oscar Wilde

▮ *The Seagull* by Anton Chekov

All Russia is our orchard. The earth is so wide, so beautiful, so full of wonderful places. [Pause]. Just think, Anya. Your grandfather, your great-grandfather and all your ancestors owned serfs, they owned human souls. Don't you see that from every cherry-tree in the orchard, from every leaf and every trunk, men and women are gazing at you? if we're to start living in the present isn't it abundantly clear that we've first got to redeem our past and make a clean break with it? And we can only redeem it by suffering and getting down to real work for a change.

The Cherry Orchard

Anton Chekhov

▌**Left to right:** First edition of *Les Fleurs du Mal* with author notes; Charles Baudelaire; Aubrey Beardsley's illustration for *Salome* by Oscar Wilde

Literary Flights of Imagination

During the Romantic period, some writers veered off the well-trodden literary path. Edgar Allan Poe (1809–1849) combined a finely honed Romantic sensibility with a taste for the macabre. He became a master of the tale of horror and invented the detective story. The poet Charles Baudelaire (1821–1867) was a devotee of Poe, and translated Poe's works into French. In his *Les Fleurs du Mal*, Baudelaire made death and decadence beautiful, and was prosecuted and fined for his efforts. Bram Stoker (1847–1912) was working as the business manager of a theater in London when he published *Dracula*, the most influential supernatural novel in history. Stoker's demonically charismatic vampire Count Dracula has inspired innumerable literary and cinematic evocations of the undead. Jules Verne (1828–1905) found the natural world more compelling than the supernatural. In novels detailing submarines and space travel, he laid the foundations for science fiction. H. G. Wells (1866–1946) used his tales of wonder to comment on politics and social issues.

Quoth the Raven, "Nevermore."

The Raven, Edgar Allan Poe

LIST OF WORKS

- ▌ *Tales of the Grotesque and Arabesque* by Edgar Allan Poe
- ▌ *Les Fleurs du Mal* by Charles Baudelaire
- ▌ *Twenty Thousand Leagues Under the Sea* by Jules Verne
- ▌ *Dracula* by Bram Stoker
- ▌ *The War of the Worlds* by H. G. Wells

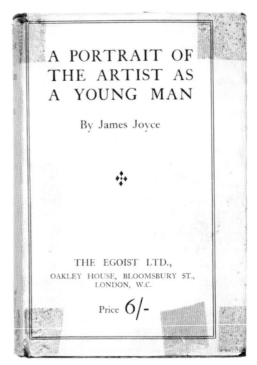

Ireland and Its Literary Diaspora

Ireland has a rich literary tradition. With their land dominated politically and economically by Britain for centuries, many Irish writers left for other places. In the late nineteenth century the Irish writers Oscar Wilde (1854–1900) and George Bernard Shaw (1856–1950) found success in England. Hoping to counteract this migratory trend, the writers of the Irish Literary Revival celebrated Ireland's Celtic traditions. John Millington Synge (1871–1909) helped establish the Abbey Theatre as the center of Irish drama, and attained notoriety with his earthy plays about Irish peasants. A theatrical associate of Synge was the poet William Butler Yeats (1865–1939), who became the first Irishman to win the Nobel Prize in Literature in 1923. James Joyce (1882–1941) left Ireland for the Continent as a young man. Though an expatriate, he set his books in Ireland, writing, "When I die Dublin will be written in my heart." While living in France, Samuel Beckett (1906–1989) helped found the "theater of the absurd."

LIST OF WORKS

▪ *Collected Poems* by William Butler Yeats

▪ *The Playboy of the Western World* by John Millington Synge

▪ *Ulysses* by James Joyce

▪ *Waiting for Godot* by Samuel Beckett

▪ *The Great Gatsby* by F. Scott Fitzgerald

THE LAKE ISLE OF INNISFREE

And I shall have some peace there,
for peace comes dropping slow,
Dropping from the veils of the morning
to where the cricket sings;
There midnight's all a glimmer,
and noon a purple glow,
And evening full of the linnet's wings.

—William Butler Yeats

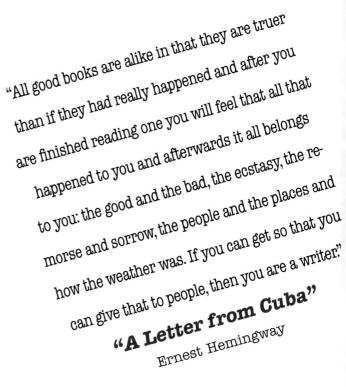

"It's because I'm alone. If I could just feel it, it would be different, because I would not be alone. But if I were not alone, everybody would know it. And he could do so much for me, and then I would not be alone. Then I could be all right alone."

As I Lay Dying
William Faulkner

"All good books are alike in that they are truer than if they had really happened and after you are finished reading one you will feel that all that happened to you and afterwards it all belongs to you: the good and the bad, the ecstasy, the remorse and sorrow, the people and the places and how the weather was. If you can get so that you can give that to people, then you are a writer."

"A Letter from Cuba"
Ernest Hemingway

Early Twentieth-Century American Writers

The poetry of Robert Frost (1874–1963) forms a transition point from nineteenth- to twentieth-century American literature. Using traditional poetic forms, Frost discovered universal themes in his rural New England surroundings. T. S. Eliot (1888–1965) embraced Modernism in his poetry. His *The Hollow Men* captured the moral bleakness of the post–World War I period with its lines "This is the way the world ends / Not with a bang but a whimper." The novelists of the 1920s captured the disillusioned mood of the time. Sinclair Lewis (1885–1951) satirized the materialistic complacency of Middle America. He became the first American to win the Nobel Prize in Literature in 1930. Ernest Hemingway (1899–1961) saw action in the Great War and then spent time as an expatriate member of the "Lost Generation." In his books he distilled the experience of morally uprooted young people, doing so with a lean, spare prose that influenced a generation of writers. William Faulkner (1897–1962) explored the dark heart of Southern culture in a brilliant series of novels.

LIST OF WORKS

- *Collected Poems of Robert Frost* by Robert Frost
- *Main Street* by Sinclair Lewis
- *The Waste Land* by T. S. Eliot
- *The Sun Also Rises* by Ernest Hemingway
- *The Sound and the Fury* by William Faulkner

The woods are lovely, dark and deep.
But I have promises to keep,
And miles to go before I sleep,
And miles to go before I sleep.

Robert Frost, "Stopping by Woods on a Snowy Evening"

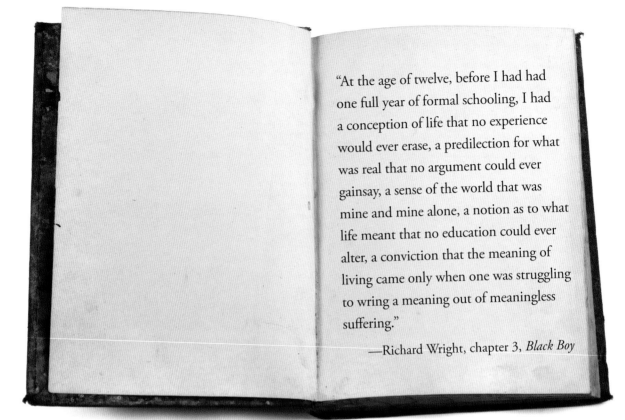

"At the age of twelve, before I had had one full year of formal schooling, I had a conception of life that no experience would ever erase, a predilection for what was real that no argument could ever gainsay, a sense of the world that was mine and mine alone, a notion as to what life meant that no education could ever alter, a conviction that the meaning of living came only when one was struggling to wring a meaning out of meaningless suffering."

—Richard Wright, chapter 3, *Black Boy*

Twentieth-Century African-American Writing

African-American writing flowered during the Harlem Renaissance of the 1920s in New York City. The poet Langston Hughes (1902–1967) gave voice to an early version of black pride, writing: "The night is beautiful / So the faces of my people." Zora Neale Hurston (1891–1960) was an anthropologist and folklorist as well as a writer. She wrote about rural African Americans as she knew them, refusing to introduce overtly political messages into her fiction, which led to criticism from some of her peers.

Richard Wright (1908–1960) embraced politics, and used his stories and novels to criticize racial inequality. Ralph Ellison (1914–1994) explored the many dilemmas facing African Americans at mid-century in his *Invisible Man*, in which his nameless protagonist travels from rural America to New York City, his existential crisis accentuated by his race. In recent decades, the poet Maya Angelou (b. 1928) and the novelist Toni Morrison (b. 1931) have achieved enormous popular as well as critical success.

LIST OF WORKS

▮ *Their Eyes Were Watching God* by Zora Neale Hurston

▮ *Native Son* by Richard Wright

▮ *Invisible Man* by Ralph Ellison

▮ *Beloved* by Toni Morrison

"At fifteen life had taught me undeni-
ably that surrender, in its place, was as
honorable as resistance, especially if one
had no choice."

—Maya Angelou,
I Know Why the Caged Bird Sings, chapter 31

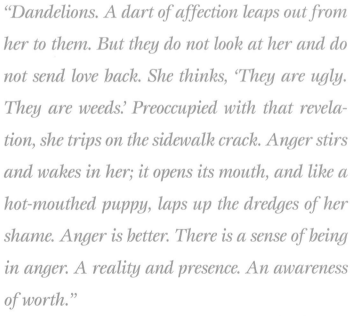

*"Dandelions. A dart of affection leaps out from
her to them. But they do not look at her and do
not send love back. She thinks, 'They are ugly.
They are weeds.' Preoccupied with that revela-
tion, she trips on the sidewalk crack. Anger stirs
and wakes in her; it opens its mouth, and like a
hot-mouthed puppy, laps up the dredges of her
shame. Anger is better. There is a sense of being
in anger. A reality and presence. An awareness
of worth."*

—Toni Morrison, *The Bluest Eye*

Twentieth-Century Latin American Literature

One of the most influential and original writers of the twentieth century was the Argentine Jorge Luis Borges (1899–1986), whose philosophically sophisticated stories could range into science fiction and often prefigured the magical realism that would be widespread in Latin American literature later in the century. Pablo Neruda (1904–1973) combined poetry with social engagement, becoming famous for his verse as well as his communism and his role in Chilean politics. In the 1960s the Latin American Boom saw an explosion of work by young experimental writers who challenged the cultural and political establishments of their homelands. The novelist Carlos Fuentes (b. 1928) explored the tangled nature of Mexican identity in his books. The Columbian Gabriel García Márquez (b. 1927) became a master of magical realism, seamlessly blending the fantastic and the quotidian in stories about the fictional town of Macondo. Mario Vargas Llosa (b. 1936) wrestled with the many forms of power and its corruption in his native Peru.

LIST OF WORKS

▮ *Twenty Love Poems and a Song of Despair* by Pablo Neruda

▮ *Ficciones* by Jorge Luis Borges

▮ *The Death of Artemio Cruz* by Carlos Fuentes

▮ *One Hundred Years of Solitude* by Gabriel García Márquez

▮ *Conversation in the Cathedral* by Mario Vargas Llosa

"The world must be all fucked up when men travel first class and literature goes as freight."

—Gabriel García Márquez,
One Hundred Years of Solitude

Eastern Literature

One Thousand and One Nights, a collection of stories, emerged in the Arab world during the Middle Ages. These tales originated as far away as India, and the framing story of the king and Scheherazade came from Persia. Some of the most famous stories, such as those of Aladdin, Ali Baba, and Sinbad the Sailor, were folktales added to the collection by European translators. Lady Murasaki's (ca. 973–ca. 1025) *The Tale of Genji,* written in early eleventh-century Japan, brilliantly portrays the lives of people at the imperial court. *The Tale of the Heike* is an epic account of the power struggle between the Taira and Minamoto clans that culminated in the Genpei War of 1180–1185. Luo Guanzhong's (ca. 1330–ca. 1400) *Romance of the Three Kingdoms* is an enormously popular historical novel about the turbulent end of the Han Dynasty. Wu Cheng'en's (ca. 1500–ca. 1582) *Journey to the West* is simultaneously an adventure story and an allegory of Buddhist enlightenment.

▌**Top to bottom:** Scenes from *Dream of the Red Chamber* by Sun Wen; Sekkan Sakurai's illustration of *Romance of the Three Kingdoms*

LIST OF WORKS

▌ *One Thousand and One Nights*

▌ *The Tale of Genji* by Murasaki Shibiku

▌ *The Tale of the Heike*

▌ *Romance of the Three Kingdoms* by Luo Guanzhong

▌ *Journey to the West* by Wu Cheng'en

▌ **Top to bottom:** Maxfield Parrish's illustration of *Ali Baba and the Forty Thieves*; a scene from *One Thousand and One Nights*, where Queen Labe unveils before King Beder

South Asian Literature

The earliest writings in Indian literature are the Vedas, religious texts composed in Sanskrit. The Rigveda was probably first composed between 1700 and 1100 B.C. The Upanishads are commentaries on the Vedas. Some of the earliest Upanishads date back to around 800 B.C. Between the sixth and first centuries B.C. two great Sanskrit epics emerged. The *Mahabharata* is an enormous poem that is framed as the story of a war between two branches of a family for control of the Kingdom of Hastinapura. But the narrative is interrupted by many digressions. The most famous is the *Bhagavad Gita*, a discussion between Krishna and Prince Arjuna before the decisive Battle of Kurukshetra about duty and the fundamental tenets of Hinduism. The *Ramayana* tells of Rama and his long struggle with the demon King Ravana. Rama is forced to undergo many tests and ordeals and overcomes all, becoming an embodiment of dharma, the Hindu exemplar of virtue.

The impact of a drop of water, a common analogy for the terms *brahman* and *atman*, used in the Upanishads

Top to bottom: A depiction of the Hindu deity Krishna; heroes of *Mahabharata*, bas relief at Angkor Wat, Cambodia

Chapter 8

Philosophy and Religion

The philosopher Socrates inspired unease among his Athenian fellow citizens. His disciple Plato called Socrates the "gadfly" of the city because of Socrates's habit of constantly raising issues that forced the Athenians to question their beliefs. Socrates's pursuit of the truth through his dialectic method of relentless argument attracted to him a number of followers from among the young men of the city. Some of these men later became leaders in the oligarchic government of the Thirty Tyrants that briefly ruled Athens after its defeat by Sparta in the Peloponnesian War. This led many Athenians to doubt Socrates's loyalty to their city's democracy, and in the year 399 B.C., Socrates was brought to trial before a jury of citizens. He was accused of corrupting the minds of the young and of "not believing in the gods of the state." Socrates vigorously defended himself, but he refused to say anything that might curry favor with the jurors. Upon being convicted, he was asked what he thought would be an appropriate sentence. He responded that he should be provided free dinners as a public benefactor. This and subsequent offers to pay a fine did nothing to mollify the angered jurors. Socrates was sentenced to death. The friends of Socrates urged him to escape, but he refused, arguing that it was unphilosophic to fear death and too late to disobey the laws of Athens. At the appointed time, he drank a cup of poisonous hemlock. Socrates died for his ideas and in doing so became a model of intellectual and moral integrity.

The Origins of Western Thought

Philosophy originated in Ancient Greece as an attempt to understand life through reason rather than faith. The first Greek philosophers sought natural explanations for the world around them. Thales believed that everything derived from water. In the same spirit, Thales's successors posited different organizing principles for physical existence, but continued to explain life in terms of natural processes. The Sophists of the fifth century B.C. were teachers of rhetoric who shifted the focus of philosophy to ethics and self-knowledge. Protagoras, for example, declared, "Man is the measure of all things." The moral relativism implicit in this teaching inspired Socrates to search for truth and virtue. He did this through a rigorous discipline of questioning. His pupil Plato developed a metaphysical doctrine that held that the material world is merely a shadow of an ultimate reality of Ideal Forms known only by the wise. Aristotle rejected his teacher Plato's metaphysics and demonstrated a wide-ranging interest in human affairs and nature.

PEOPLE OF NOTE

▮ Thales (ca. 624–ca. 546 B.C.)

▮ Anaximander (ca. 610–ca. 546 B.C.)

▮ Anaximenes (ca. 585–ca. 528 B.C.)

▮ Xenophanes (ca. 570–ca. 475 B.C.)

▮ Pythagoras (ca. 570–495 B.C.)

▮ Heraclitus (ca. 535–475 B.C.)

▮ Parmenides (ca. 510–ca. 450 B.C.)

▮ Anaxagoras (ca. 500–428 B.C.)

▮ Empedocles (ca. 490–ca. 430 B.C.)

▮ Protagoras (ca. 490–420 B.C.)

▮ Socrates (ca. 469–399 B.C.)

▮ Democritus (ca. 460–ca. 370 B.C.)

▮ Plato (ca. 427–ca. 347 B.C.)

▮ Aristotle (384–322 B.C.)

▮ Epicurus (341–270 B.C.)

▮ Zeno (ca. 334–262 B.C.)

▮ **This page left to right:** Socrates; Aristotle; *St. Paul Preaching in Athens* by Raphael; **Opposite page:** excerpt from *Sophist* by Plato; Plato addressing his students

THEODORUS. Here we are, Socrates, true to our agreement of yesterday; and we bring with us a stranger from Elea, who is a disciple of Parmenides and Zeno, and a true philosopher.

SOCRATES. Is he not rather a god, Theodorus, who comes to us in the disguise of a stranger? For Homer says that all the gods, and especially the god of strangers, are companions of the meek and just, and visit the good and evil among men. And may not your companion be one of those higher powers, a cross-examining deity, who has come to spy out our weakness in argument, and to cross-examine us?

THEOD. Nay, Socrates, he is not one of the disputatious sort—he is too good for that. And, in my opinion, he is not a god at all; but divine he certainly is, for this is a title which I should give to all philosophers.

SOC. Capital, my friend! and I may add that they are almost as hard to be discerned as the gods. For the true philosophers, and such as are not merely made up for the occasion, appear in various forms unrecognized by the ignorance of men, and they "hover about cities," as Homer declares, looking from above upon human life; and some think nothing of them, and others can never think enough; and sometimes they appear as statesmen, and sometimes as sophists; and then, again, to many they seem to be no better than madmen. I should like to ask our Eleatic friend, if he would tell us, what is thought about them in Italy, and to whom the terms are applied.

THEOD. What terms?

SOC. Sophist, statesman, philosopher.

THEOD. What is your difficulty about them, and what made you ask?

Ancient Eastern Thought

Hindu scriptural writings and commentaries are among the world's oldest philosophical writings, going back 3,000 years. Hinduism is believed to have been practiced at least 7,000 years ago. The Hindu tradition is richly diverse, but all strains of Hinduism emphasize the significance of a transcendent order in the universe and the importance of recognizing and living in accord with natural law. Mahavira laid down the principles of Jainism, stressing the importance of nonviolence. Siddhartha Gautama Buddha, a prince who renounced his riches, promoted the Noble Eightfold Path to enlightenment, founding one of the world's great religions, Buddhism. In China, Confucius created an ethical system extolling personal virtue and social benevolence. Taoism, associated with Laozi (also spelled Lao-Tzu), focuses on the necessity of achieving harmony with the inner essence of life. The Legalists were worldly thinkers interested in the primacy of law in securing the rule of the Qin monarchs. Confucianism, Taoism, and Legalism shaped Chinese thought for centuries to come.

▌**This page top to bottom:** Confucius; Temple of Heaven, Beijing China; **Opposite page left to right:** Mandala with the Hindu god Lord Ganesh as a central design; Buddha face, Ayutthaya, Thailand

PEOPLE OF NOTE

▮ Mahavira (ca. 599–ca. 527 B.C.)

▮ Siddhartha Gautama Buddha (ca. 563–ca. 483 B.C.)

▮ Confucius (551–479 B.C.)

▮ Laozi (ca. 500s B.C.)

▮ Mozi (ca. 470–ca. 391 B.C.)

▮ Shang Yang (390–338 B.C.)

▮ Mencius (ca. 372–ca. 289 B.C.)

▮ Zhuangzi (ca. 369–ca. 286 B.C.)

▮ Xunzi (ca. 312–ca. 230 B.C.)

▮ Han Fei (ca. 280–233 B.C.)

▮ Li Si (ca. 280–208 B.C.)

Philosophy in the Middle Ages

Medieval philosophy was shaped by the cultural dominance of Christianity. For medieval thinkers, philosophy was the handmaiden of theology; they used logic and elements drawn from Classical philosophy to help them illuminate questions of religious significance. Augustine set the tone for medieval philosophy by firmly subordinating reason to faith; he wrote, "Understand in order that you may believe, believe in order that you may understand." In this spirit, Anselm of Canterbury used reason and logic in his ontological argument for the existence of God. In the late eleventh and early twelfth centuries, the great medieval universities began to appear.

▌Anselm of Canterbury

▐ Scene from a medieval university classroom

PEOPLE OF NOTE

▐ Augustine (A.D. 354–430)

▐ Boethius (ca. 480–ca. 524)

▐ Johannes Scotus Eriugena (ca. 815–ca. 877)

▐ Anselm of Canterbury (ca. 1033–1109)

ABÉLARD AND HÉLOÏSE.

The Scholastics

Peter Abelard was a brilliant teacher during the twelfth-century explosion of learning who advocated the use of logic in academic disputation, though he is most famous now for his tragic love affair with his pupil Heloise. In the universities, Scholastic philosophy emphasized a rigorous method of argument and counterargument to resolve questions. The greatest of the Scholastics was Thomas Aquinas, who in his *Summa Theologica* created a monument to medieval learning.

PEOPLE OF NOTE

▌ Peter Abelard (1079–1142)

▌ Albertus Magnus (Albert the Great; ca. 1200–1280)

▌ Thomas Aquinas (1225–1274)

▌ William of Occam (or "Ockham"; ca. 1248–ca. 1348)

▌ John Duns Scotus (ca. 1265–1308)

▌ Nicholas of Cusa (1401–1464)

▌ **This page top to bottom:** Abelard and Heloise; picture of a medieval school from a fourteenth-century illuminated manuscript; **Opposite page:** Thomas Aquinas

Early Modern Philosophy and the Age of Reason

As a result of the Scientific Revolution of the sixteenth and seventeenth centuries, philosophy moved beyond the rigid categories of Scholasticism and embraced a new faith in reason and experimentation. Francis Bacon captured the new intellectual mood with his *Great Instauration*, a remodeling of human thought based upon an inductive methodology. Bacon was not the only thinker looking for a new beginning. René Descartes revolutionized philosophy by systematically doubting everything that he knew. Assuming that knowledge could only come from reason, he arrived at his famous starting point, "I think, therefore I am," and began rebuilding his understanding of the world on rationalist grounds. John Locke, in his political philosophy, provided a defense of natural rights and limited government, anticipating the next century's American Declaration of Independence.

The eighteenth-century Enlightenment continued this intellectual renewal. Thinkers celebrated human rationality, giving rise to the phrase "the Age of Reason." Increasing knowledge of the laws of nature and attendant improvements in technology inspired a robust belief in human progress. Writers as diverse as the historian Edward Gibbon and the political philosopher Jean-Jacques Rousseau shared a confidence that humanity's best days lay ahead. Public intellectuals, known in France as the *philosophes*, worked to disseminate the insights of the Scientific Revolution. In addition to his scathing critiques of contemporary politics and religion, Voltaire wrote a popular introduction to the work of Isaac Newton, while Denis Diderot led the team of writers that produced the *Encyclopédie* (1751–1772).

PEOPLE OF NOTE

- Francis Bacon (1561–1626)
- Thomas Hobbes (1588–1679)
- Pierre Gassendi (1592–1655)
- René Descartes (1596–1650)
- Blaise Pascal (1623–1662)
- Baruch Spinoza (1632–1677)
- John Locke (1632–1704)
- Nicolas Malebranche (1638–1715)
- Gottfried Leibniz (1646–1716)
- Pierre Bayle (1647–1706)
- François-Marie Arouet (Voltaire) (1694–1778)
- Denis Diderot (1711–1784)
- Jean-Jacques Rousseau (1712–1778)
- Claude Adrien Helvétius (1715–1771)
- Jean le Rond d'Alembert (1717–1783)
- Paul Heinrich Dietrich, Baron d'Holbach (1723–1789)
- Edward Gibbon (1737–1794)
- Thomas Paine (1737–1809)
- Nicolas de Caritat, Marquis de Condorcet (1743–1794)
- Mary Wollstonecraft (1759–1797)

Jean-Jacques Rousseau

I THINK, THEREFORE I AM

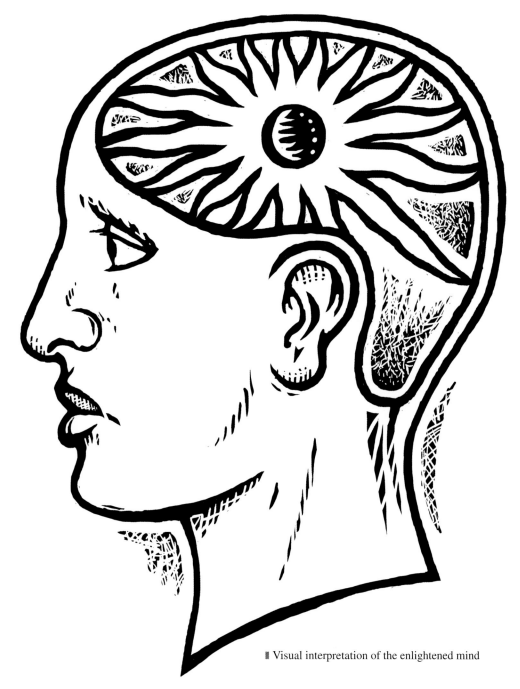

❚ Visual interpretation of the enlightened mind

American Philosophy

America in the eighteenth century was influenced by the European Enlightenment. Benjamin Franklin became famous on both sides of the Atlantic for his scientific writings and especially for his experiments with electricity. In addition to being a widely respected sage, Franklin was an active statesman who played a leading role in the struggle for American independence.

The Founding Fathers of the United States were deeply indebted to the writings of political philosophers such as Locke. Their genius was to take ideas about natural rights and separation of powers and embed them in enduring political structures. The Constitution of the United States is the oldest still-functioning constitution in the world.

American Romanticism in the nineteenth century was expressed by the Transcendentalist writers Ralph Waldo Emerson and Henry David Thoreau, who celebrated nature and self-reliance. William James distilled the practical side of American thought in his philosophy of Pragmatism, judging ideas by their usefulness.

⫾ Replica of Thoreau's cabin at Walden Woods © RhythmicQuietude at en.wikipedia; **inset:** cabin interior

PEOPLE OF NOTE

▍ Benjamin Franklin (1706–1790)

▍ John Adams (1735–1826)

▍ Thomas Jefferson (1743–1826)

▍ James Madison (1751–1836)

▍ Alexander Hamilton (1755–1804)

▍ Ralph Waldo Emerson (1803–1882)

▍ Henry David Thoreau (1817–1862)

▍ Charles Sanders Peirce (1839–1914)

▍ William James (1842–1910)

▍ John Dewey (1859–1952)

▍ **Top to bottom:** U.S. Constitution; Benjamin Franklin and the kite experiment

Nineteenth-Century German Thought

The German Idealist philosophers wrestled with the legacy of Immanuel Kant: If objects were known only by the mind's experience of them, then how could one approach the "thing in itself"? Georg Wilhelm Friedrich Hegel believed that he transcended the mind/matter dilemma by arguing that consciousness developed over time in a dialectical engagement with the world. He held that Absolute Spirit was becoming manifest through a historical process. Karl Marx adapted Hegel's dialectic to his materialistic and economic understanding of history. Instead of the triumph of Absolute Spirit, Marx thought history would end with the advent of communism. Søren Kierkegaard and Friedrich Nietzsche rejected systematic philosophy and focused on the individual's need to make hard choices in a demanding world. Nietzsche declared, "God is dead." Consequently, humanity, bereft of moral absolutes, must move "beyond good and evil," creating new values and embracing the "will to power."

▌**Top to bottom:** Friedrich Nietzsche; Karl Marx

PEOPLE OF NOTE

- Jeremy Bentham (1748–1832)

- Johann Gottlieb Fichte (1762–1814)

- Georg Wilhelm Friedrich Hegel (1770–1831)

- Friedrich Wilhelm Joseph Schelling (1775–1854)

- Arthur Schopenhauer (1788–1860)

- Auguste Comte (1798–1857)

- John Stuart Mill (1806–1873)

- Søren Kierkegaard (1813–1855)

- Karl Marx (1818–1883)

- Friedrich Nietzsche (1844–1900)

▌ Hegel with his students

▌**Left to right:** Simone de Beauvoir; Jean-Paul Sartre; Noam Chomsky; Hannah Arendt; Michel Foucault

Twentieth-Century Philosophy

There were two main approaches to philosophy in the early twentieth century. The Analytic philosophers rejected Hegelian idealism, instead building on innovations in formal logic. The Analytic perspective predominated in Great Britain and the United States, where philosophers such as Bertrand Russell sought to clarify traditional philosophic problems by recasting linguistic propositions in logical terms. The Logical Positivists went further, arguing that any statement that could not be verified empirically was meaningless, reducing philosophical analysis to an exercise in defining concepts. Continental philosophy explored lived experience, and eventually was more heavily influenced by the traumas of World Wars I and II and totalitarianism. Edmund Husserl attempted to get beyond traditional idealism by recognizing the intentionality of human experience, noting that consciousness is always directed at an object. Husserl's phenomenological method undergirded the existential philosophies of Martin Heidegger and Jean-Paul Sartre, who grappled with the problem of living in a godless and meaningless universe. Sartre emphasized human freedom in the face of nothingness.

Existentialism appealed to a generation scarred by World War II. Simone de Beauvoir extended existential analysis to the situation faced by women, pioneering feminist philosophy. Structuralism argued that the products of human culture are best understood as manifestations of underlying mental constructs. Structuralists such as the anthropologist Claude Lévi-Strauss were very influential in the humanities and social sciences. Noam Chomsky came to prominence by critiquing linguistic structuralism. Michel Foucault was heavily influenced by Structuralism in his early "archaeological" studies of the concepts that shaped the growth of the medical profession and the modern understanding of madness. However, in his later works Foucault focused more on the ways ideas were used to justify power, and as a self-described Nietzschean, he rejected any order or intrinsic meaning in life. Jacques Derrida and the Deconstructionists also refused to acknowledge any authoritative truths; cultural products were simply manifestations of various, often oppressive, ideologies.

"Wherever there is power, there is a temptation to encourage credulity in those who are subject to the power in question."

— BERTRAND RUSSELL

PEOPLE OF NOTE

- Gottlob Frege (1848–1925)
- Edmund Husserl (1859–1938)
- Henri Bergson (1859–1941)
- Alfred North Whitehead (1861–1947)
- Bertrand Russell (1872–1970)
- George Edward Moore (1873–1958)

- Karl Jaspers (1883–1969)
- Ludwig Wittgenstein (1889–1951)
- Martin Heidegger (1889–1976)
- Hans-Georg Gadamer (1900–2002)
- Jean-Paul Sartre (1905–1980)
- Hannah Arendt (1906–1975)
- Simone de Beauvoir (1908–1986)

- Claude Lévi-Strauss (1908–2009)
- A. J. Ayer (1910–1989)
- Michel Foucault (1926–1984)
- Noam Chomsky (b. 1928)
- Jürgen Habermas (b. 1929)
- Jacques Derrida (1930–2004)
- Richard Rorty (1931–2007)

Chapter 9

Science and Mathematics

According to an old story, King Hiero of Syracuse gave a goldsmith a quantity of gold to make a crown. When the goldsmith presented the king with the finished crown, Hiero grew suspicious that he had been cheated. The crown weighed the same as the gold that had been given to the goldsmith, but something about the crown seemed wrong to the king. Hiero asked the great scientist and mathematician Archimedes to determine the truth about the golden crown. Archimedes spent many hours pondering the puzzle. One day he was thinking about the problem while he was preparing for a bath. The tub had been filled to the brim, and when Archimedes slipped in, water sloshed over the edge. When Archimedes saw this, he suddenly realized that he had discovered a way to measure the amount of gold in the crown. "Eureka!" he cried, "I have found it!" What Archimedes realized was that different materials have different volumes. The same weight of gold or brass will displace different amounts of water. Archimedes set up an experiment. He filled two bowls of the same size with water. Into one he placed the crown, and into the other an ingot of gold of the same weight. He measured the displaced water, and proved that the gold in the crown had been adulterated with cheaper metals. Confronted with this evidence, the goldsmith confessed his theft. Archimedes's famous "Eureka!" moment has become paradigmatic of both the joy of scientific discovery and the practical benefits such knowledge provides.

Cosmology

Human beings have studied the heavens for thousands of years. The ancient Babylonians and Egyptians made precise observations of planets and stars. Greek astronomers laid the foundations of astronomy as a science in the West, combining observation with sophisticated mathematical modeling. Aristarchus of Samos was an early proponent of a heliocentric understanding of the solar system, while Eratosthenes made a remarkably accurate estimate of the Earth's circumference. Claudius Ptolemy's treatise on celestial motion, based on a geocentric model of the universe, dominated astronomical thinking for 1,200 years. Nicolaus Copernicus, a Polish priest, upended Ptolemaic astronomy with his mathematical defense of a sun-centered planetary system. Galileo Galilei experimentally confirmed the Copernican theory, using an early telescope. Johannes Kepler followed this up with the counterintuitive proof that the planets orbited the sun in elliptical rather than circular paths. The astronomical revolution was completed by Isaac Newton, who explained these elliptical orbits through his law of universal gravitation.

Modern cosmology is rooted in the theoretical and experimental reactions to Albert Einstein's Theory of General Relativity. Einstein's theory posited a dynamic cosmological model, in which the universe could be expanding and contracting. Einstein himself preferred a static model of the universe. The cosmological implications of Einstein's theory were worked out by other men in the Friedmann–Lemaître–Robertson–Walker metric. In 1912, Vesto Slipher noticed spectral redshifts in spiral nebulae, indicating that they were moving away from our terrestrial point of reference. Georges Lemaître, a Catholic priest as well as an astronomer, hypothesized that Slipher's observations meant that the universe had begun as a "creation-like" explosion, thus propounding the first version of the "big bang" theory. Edwin Hubble discovered that spiral nebulae were actually galaxies, and provided empirical support for the "big bang" understanding of an expanding universe. Stephen Hawking and Roger Penrose demonstrated the possibility of singularities within the framework of general relativity.

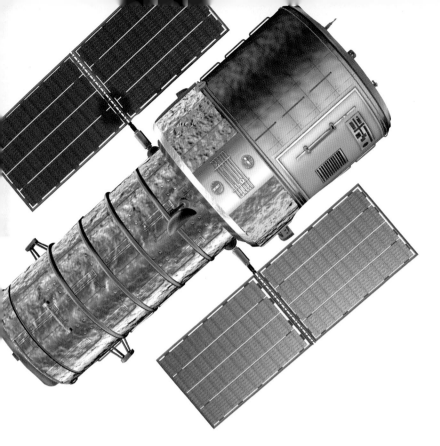

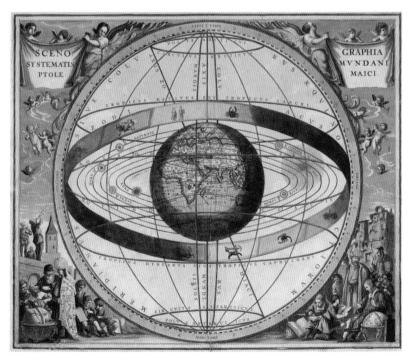

Top to bottom: Hubble telescope; Andreas Cellarius, illustration of the Ptolemaic System

Physics: Then and Now

The ancient Greeks wanted to understand the natural world and its place in the cosmos. In addition to studying the stars, they explored physical processes around them. Archimedes combined scientific research with a gift for practical engineering. He reportedly remarked, "Give me a place to stand, and I shall move the Earth with a lever." Archimedes also laid the foundations of hydrostatics and invented the screw pump. Arab and medieval European philosophers were content to ponder and elaborate on the intellectual legacy left by the Greeks. This changed with the Scientific Revolution of the sixteenth and seventeenth centuries. Galileo Galilei was an early pioneer of the experimental method. His example was soon followed by others. Royally sponsored scientific institutions such as the Royal Society in Britain and the Academy of Sciences in France promoted the experimental approach to learning.

In the late nineteenth century, the accepted understanding of the physical world began to be challenged by developments in thermodynamics. New insights into energy began to undermine mechanistic models of material interaction. James Clerk Maxwell demonstrated that electromagnetic fields explained such diverse phenomena as electricity and magnetism. The Michelson-Morley experiment on the speed of light laid the foundation for relativity theory. The discovery and investigation of radiation helped clarify atomic structure. Max Planck pioneered quantum theory while explaining the emission of radiation by heated objects. Albert Einstein set the seal on the new physics with his Theory of General Relativity, which, among other things, posited the interchangeability of mass and energy. Niels Bohr provided a model of the atom with a positively charged nucleus surrounded by negatively charged electrons that shaped atomic theory. These discoveries opened up the possibility of human control of atomic energy, but quantum mechanics raised fundamental questions about the ability to measure present and future positions of subatomic particles.

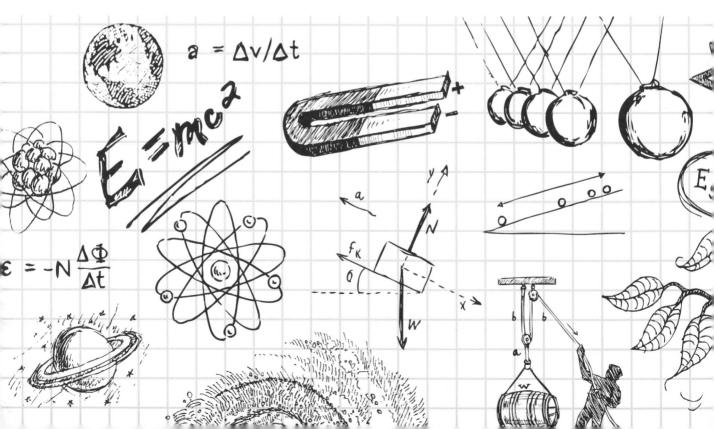

PEOPLE OF NOTE

- Archimedes (ca. 287–212 B.C.)
- Christiaan Huygens (1629–1695)
- Robert Hooke (1635–1703)
- Daniel Bernoulli (1700–1782)
- Pierre-Simon Laplace (1749–1827)
- John Dalton (1766–1844)
- Michael Faraday (1791–1867)
- James Prescott Joule (1818–1889)
- Hermann von Helmholtz (1821–1894)
- William Thomson, 1st Baron Kelvin (1824–1907)
- James Clerk Maxwell (1831–1879)
- Albert Abraham Michelson (1852–1931)
- J. J. Thomson (1856–1940)
- Max Planck (1858–1947)
- Marie Curie (1867–1934)
- Ernest Rutherford (1871–1937)
- Albert Einstein (1879–1955)
- Niels Bohr (1885–1962)
- Werner Heisenberg (1901–1976)
- Richard Feynman (1918–1988)

Left to right: Archimedes's screw; manuscript of *Horologium* by Christiaan Huygens

Medicine and Biology

The ancient Greeks worshiped Asclepius, the god of healing. At the temples of Asclepius, patients with a wide variety of ailments were treated. Eventually, physicians such as Hippocrates began to systematize medicine into a science, writing extensively on symptoms, diagnoses, and treatments. Hippocrates also pioneered medical ethics with his Hippocratic Oath, versions of which are still in use today. Linked to the ancient concern for the human body was an interest in understanding the natural world. The philosopher Aristotle and naturalists like Pliny the Elder wrote extensively on plants and animals, though generally from a descriptive rather than genuinely empirical method. A more rigorous approach to medical and biological knowledge came with the Scientific Revolution. Andreas Vesalius's dissections furthered knowledge of the human body, while Antonie van Leeuwenhoek's microscope opened up a new world. Carl Linnaeus helped lay the foundation of modern biological science with his system of classifying the natural world.

PEOPLE OF NOTE

- Hippocrates (ca. 460–ca. 370 B.C.)

- Pliny the Elder (23–79)

- Galen (129–ca. 200)

- Avicenna (ca. 980–1037)

- Andreas Vesalius (1514–1564)

- William Harvey (1578–1657)

- Antonie van Leeuwenhoek (1632–1723)

- Carl Linnaeus (1707–1778)

- Georges-Louis Leclerc, Comte de Buffon (1707–1788)

- Edward Jenner (1749–1823)

Opposite page: A page from Linnaeus's thesis, *Praeludia Sponsaliorum Plantarum*; **This page top to bottom:** Leeuwenhoek microscope; *The Cow-Pock* by James Gillray depicts Edward Jenner vaccinating patients who feared it would make them grow cowlike parts on their bodies © Library of Congress

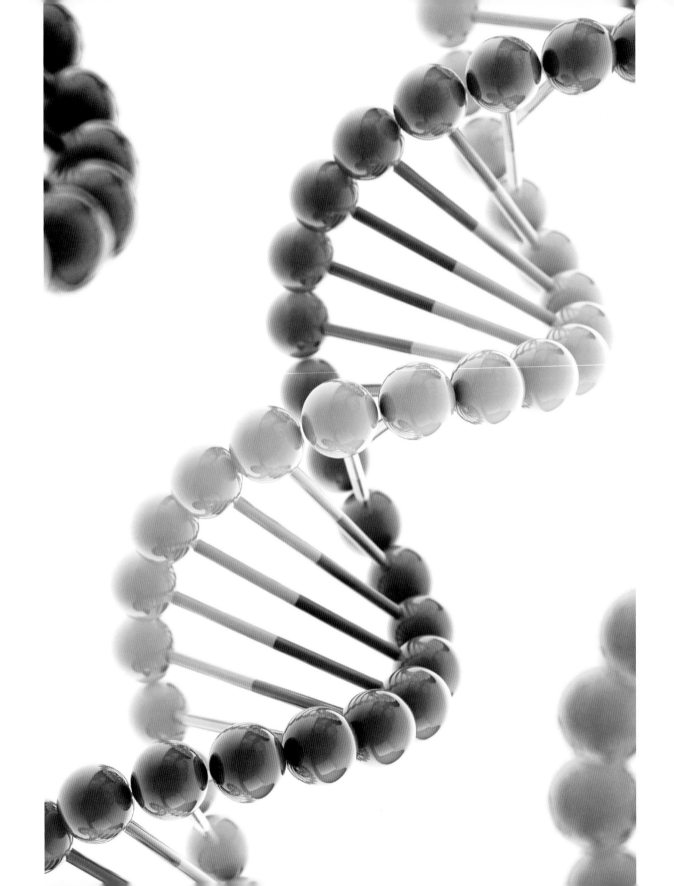

The Darwinian Decision

Medical advances in the nineteenth century were spurred by discoveries in chemistry and biology. Scientific standards were established for laboratory work. Louis Pasteur typified the new scientific approach to medical research, helping solidify the germ theory of disease. Pasteur's insights inspired Joseph Lister to promote the use of antiseptics in surgery. Biological science was revolutionized by evolutionary theory. Jean-Baptiste Lamarck proposed an early version of this by arguing that acquired characteristics could be inherited. The geological work of Charles Lyell, correspondence with fellow biologist Alfred Russel Wallace, and the results of his own research, led Charles Darwin to propose the theory of natural selection in his *On the Origin of Species* (1859). Gregor Mendel provided evidence of the mechanics of evolution with his groundbreaking studies in genetics. Years later, this line of research would lead Francis Crick and James D. Watson to unravel the structure of DNA.

PEOPLE OF NOTE

- Antoine Lavoisier (1743–1794)
- Jean-Baptiste Lamarck (1744–1829)
- Alexander von Humboldt (1769–1859)
- Charles Darwin (1809–1882)
- Gregor Mendel (1822–1884)
- Louis Pasteur (1822–1895)
- Alfred Russel Wallace (1823–1913)
- Joseph Lister (1827–1912)
- Francis Crick (1916–2004)
- James D. Watson (b. 1928)

This page: Photograph of the frontispiece of *Journal of Researches* by Charles Darwin published around 1890; **Opposite page:** Model of a DNA strand

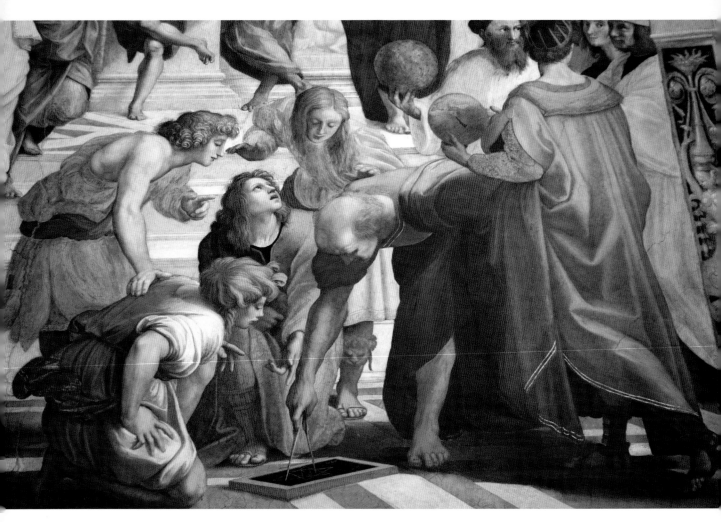

Mathematics

Mathematics has deep roots in Western civilization. The Babylonians developed a sexagesimal, or base-60, numerical system from which comes our use of 60 to measure time and the 360 degrees in a circle. Egyptian mathematics helped raise the pyramids and other great monuments. The Greeks advanced mathematical reasoning, arriving deductively at proofs for problems. Pythagoras used mathematics as the foundation of a philosophical worldview, while Hipparchus used mathematics to support astronomy. Archimedes combined mathematics with engineering and calculated the value of *pi*. Mathematicians like Euclid and Apollonius of Perga left work in geometry and conics that we use today. The Persian mathematician Muhammad ibn Musa al-Khwarizmi played a key role in passing algebra to medieval Europe. During the Scientific Revolution, many great thinkers combined mathematics with other inquiries. Descartes pioneered analytic geometry as well as philosophy, while calculus was jointly created by the scientist Isaac Newton and the philosopher Gottfried Wilhelm Leibniz.

PEOPLE OF NOTE

▮ Euclid (ca. 360–ca. 280 B.C.)

▮ Apollonius of Perga (ca. 262–ca. 190 B.C.)

▮ Muhammad ibn Musa al-Khwarizmi (ca. 780–ca. 850)

▮ Leonardo Fibonacci (ca. 1170–ca. 1250)

▮ Pierre de Fermat (ca. 1601–1665)

▮ Leonhard Euler (1707–1783)

▮ Joseph-Louis Lagrange (1736–1813)

▮ Carl Friedrich Gauss (1777–1855)

▮ Bernhard Riemann (1826–1866)

▮ Georg Cantor (1845–1918)

▮ **Opposite page:** Ptolemy and Strabo in *The School of Athens* by Raphael; **This page top to bottom:** Fibonacci pattern in a nautilus shell; Gottfried Wilhelm Leibniz

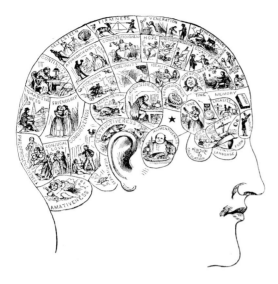

Behavioral Sciences

As the natural sciences went from one triumph to another in the nineteenth century, many began to wonder whether the human psyche and human culture could be explained with the same kind of precision as the movement of the heavens or a chemical reaction. Wilhelm Wundt inaugurated the scientific study of human psychology in 1879 when he established a research laboratory at the University of Leipzig. The study of psychology soon spread, and G. Stanley Hall and the philosopher William James were instrumental in establishing the discipline in the United States. American psychologists John B. Watson and B. F. Skinner promoted behaviorism, which held that all behaviors are the result of conditioning. Sigmund Freud pioneered psychoanalysis in Vienna, from whence it spread around the globe and attracted distinguished practitioners, notably Carl Jung. Freud argued that human behavior was compelled by unconscious and irrational drives. Anthropology emerged as the study of humanity, and scholars like Franz Boas, Margaret Mead, and Clifford Geertz developed compelling interpretations of human culture.

▌**Top to bottom:** Illustration from an 1876 issue of the *Phrenological Journal*; B. F. Skinner and his teaching machine

■ **Left to right:** Sigmund Freud; Freudian cartoon; Margaret Mead; Carl Gustav Jung

PEOPLE OF NOTE

■ Wilhelm Wundt (1832–1920)

■ G. Stanley Hall (1844–1924)

■ Sigmund Freud (1856–1939)

■ Franz Boas (1858–1942)

■ Carl Jung (1875–1961)

■ John B. Watson (1878–1958)

■ Jean Piaget (1896–1980)

■ Margaret Mead (1901–1978)

■ B. F. Skinner (1904–1990)

■ Clifford Geertz (1926–2006)

Chapter 10

Lifestyle

Henry Sands Brooks opened a men's clothing store in Manhattan on April 7, 1818. His intent was "to make and deal only in merchandise of the finest body, to sell it at a fair profit and to deal with people who seek and appreciate such merchandise." The firm became Brooks Brothers when the founder's three sons took over in 1850. Brooks Brothers combined an upscale approach to business with innovative marketing, including the invention of the "off the rack" ready-made suit. During the Civil War, profits trumped quality when it came to the masses. Brooks Brothers sold the government thousands of uniforms made of a shredded and pressed fabric known as "shoddy" that disintegrated in the rain. As war profiteers, the Brooks Brothers were in good company, and the firm suffered no adverse consequences for the ersatz clothing it inflicted on ordinary Union soldiers. In 1898, Theodore Roosevelt turned to Brooks Brothers to tailor the dress uniform he wore as he charged into the Spanish American War. As purveyors of fine clothing to the American elite, Brooks Brothers took the lead in exposing American men to such sartorial advances as button-down collars on dress shirts, argyle socks, and seersucker suits. Celebrities as diverse as Cary Grant and Andy Warhol patronized Brooks Brothers, and for over 150 years, politicians have been drawn to the traditional elegance epitomized by the firm. Both Abraham Lincoln and Barack Obama were inaugurated wearing Brooks Brothers coats. Through the ups and downs of nearly two centuries, Henry Sands Brooks's dream of a fashionable and fashion-setting clothier has endured. Brooks Brothers today is an institution, a commercial brand that has the enviable distinction of being simultaneously a noun and an adjective.

The Lifestyles of the Cultured

The wealthy have always been distinguished by the luxury goods that they have been able to afford. For most of history, conspicuous consumption has been a mark of aristocratic superiority. Ancient rulers were buried with many of their treasures, and the tomb of the pharaoh Tutankhamun (King Tut) revealed some of the sumptuous luxuries he enjoyed in life. Cleopatra once impressed Mark Antony by dropping a valuable pearl into vinegar and, once it dissolved, drinking it. The excesses of ancient Rome are legendary. Petronius, in his novel *Satyricon*, has the rich freedman Trimalchio order that any silverware dropped on the floor from his table be thrown out. In our own time, real estate mogul Donald Trump bought a 757 jet with gold-plated fixtures. Harrods, the British department store, caters to an exclusive clientele with luxury items that have ranged from $165 million yachts to a bathtub carved out of a solid piece of rock crystal that retailed for $790,000.

▌*The Banquet of Cleopatra* by Giambattista Tiepolo

▌Generally considered the most expensive dog breed in the world, the Alsatian (German shepherd) can fetch between $3,000 and $24,000.

Food and Fashion

Human beings have long been subject to the whims of fashion. The evolution of women's hairstyles in ancient Rome can be traced through coins and portrait busts. The fourth-century A.D. Roman historian Ammianus Marcellinus ridiculed the contemporary taste for fine-textured fringed cloaks that wearers whipped about with their left hands. The modern fashion industry emerged in Paris at the turn of the twentieth century. Soon dress buyers in Middle America were imitating styles that originated with designers such as Coco Chanel (1883–1971). Fashionable people needed fashionable places to go. In late-nineteenth- and early-twentieth-century New York City, the well-to-do could take in a show and then head to dinner at Delmonico's, where they rubbed shoulders with Diamond Jim Brady, J. P. Morgan, Lillian Russell, or Theodore Roosevelt. At Delmonico's they might enjoy such signature dishes as Lobster Newburg, Eggs Benedict, and the famed Delmonico steak.

Menu for a 1916 dinner at Delmonico's

Photo and Illustration Credits